Harwood Fundamentals of Pure and Applied Economics

URBAN DYNAMICS AND URBAN EXTERNALITIES

hwap

Routledge
Taylor & Francis Group
LONDON AND NEW YORK

FUNDAMENTALS OF PURE AND APPLIED ECONOMICS

REGIONAL & URBAN ECONOMICS I
In 4 Volumes

I	Location Theory	*Gabszewicz et al.*
II	Urban Public Finance	*Wildasin*
III	Urban Dynamics and Urban Externalities	*Miyao and Kanemoto*
IV	Systems of Cities and Facility Location	*Hansen et al.*

URBAN DYNAMICS AND URBAN EXTERNALITIES

TAKAHIRO MIYAO AND
YOSHITSUGU KANEMOTO

Routledge
Taylor & Francis Group
LONDON AND NEW YORK

First published in 1987 by
Harwood Academic Publishers GmbH

Reprinted in 2001 by
Routledge
2 Park Square, Milton Park, Abingdon, Oxon, OX14 4RN
711 Third Avenue, New York, NY 10017

Transferred to Digital Printing 2007

Routledge is an imprint of the Taylor & Francis Group

First issued in paperback 2013

The publishers have made every effort to contact authors/copyright holders of the works reprinted in *Harwood Fundamentals of Pure & Applied Economics*. This has not been possible in every case, however, and we would welcome correspondence from those individuals/companies we have been unable to trace.

These reprints are taken from original copies of each book. in many cases the condition of these originals is not perfect. the publisher has gone to great lengths to ensure the quality of these reprints, but wishes to point out that certain characteristics of the original copies will, of necessity, be apparent in reprints thereof.

British Library Cataloguing in Publication Data
A CIP catalogue record for this book
is available from the British Library

ISBN13: 978-0-415-27474-6 (HB)

ISBN13: 978-0-415-86633-0 (PB)

Urban Dynamics and Urban Externalities

Takahiro Miyao
University of Southern California, USA
and University of Tsukuba, Japan

and

Yoshitsugu Kanemoto
University of Tsukuba, Japan

A volume in the Regional and Urban Economics section
edited by
Richard Arnott
Queen's University, Canada

harwood academic publishers
chur · london · paris · new york

Harwood Academic Publishers

Post Office Box 197
London WC2E 9PX
England

58, rue Lhomond
75005 Paris
France

Post Office Box 786
Cooper Station
New York, NY 10276
United States of America

Library of Congress Cataloging-in-Publication Data

Miyao, Takahiro.
Urban dynamics and urban externalities.

(Fundamentals of pure and applied economics; vol. 11.
Regional and urban economics section, ISSN 0191-1708)
Includes bibliographies and indexes.
1. Population density. 2. Externalities (Economics)
3. Urban economics. I. Kanemoto, Yoshitsugu. II. Title.
III. Series: Fundamentals of pure and applied economics;
vol. 11. IV. Series: Fundamentals of pure and
applied economics. Regional and urban economics section.
HB2161.M595 1986 330.9173'2 86-25629
ISBN 3-7186-0333-0

Contents

Introduction to the Series

Drawing on a personal network, an economist can still relatively easily stay well informed in the narrow field in which he works, but to keep up with the development of economics as a whole is a much more formidable challenge. Economists are confronted with difficulties associated with the rapid development of their discipline. There is a risk of "balkanisation" in economics, which may not be favorable to its development.

Fundamentals of Pure and Applied Economics has been created to meet this problem. The discipline of economics has been subdivided into sections (listed inside). These sections include short books, each surveying the state of the art in a given area.

Each book starts with the basic elements and goes as far as the most advanced results. Each should be useful to professors needing material for lectures, to graduate students looking for a global view of a particular subject, to professional economists wishing to keep up with the development of their science, and to researchers seeking convenient information on questions that incidentally appear in their work.

Each book is thus a presentation of the state of the art in a particular field rather than a step-by-step analysis of the development of the literature. Each is a high-level presentation but accessible to anyone with a solid background in economics, whether engaged in business, government, international organizations, teaching, or research in related fields.

Three aspects of *Fundamentals of Pure and Applied Economics* should be emphasized:

—First, the project covers the whole field of economics, not only theoretical or mathematical economics.

—Second, the project is open-ended and the number of books is not predetermined. If new interesting areas appear, they will generate additional books.
—Last, all the books making up each section will later be grouped to constitute one or several volumes of an Encyclopedia of Economics.

The editors of the sections are outstanding economists who have selected as authors for the series some of the finest specialists in the world.

J. Lesourne *H. Sonnenschein*

Urban Growth and Dynamics

TAKAHIRO MIYAO

Institute of Socio-Economic Planning, University of Tsukuba, Ibaraki, Japan and Department of Economics, University of Southern California, Los Angeles, CA, U.S.A.

1. INTRODUCTION

This survey reviews recent developments in dynamic models of urban production and residential activities. In fact, much of the theoretical analysis of urban dynamics has been attempted only recently, and construction of elaborate models which pay explicit attention to both time and space has just begun among relatively young researchers in the field. It could still be too early to review the literature on this rapidly advancing subject and to sort out net contributions of various studies from a long-term viewpoint. Surveying the current state of the art on urban growth and dynamics at this juncture, however, may be worthwhile, since it can give some helpful ideas and directions to those who plan to study some dynamic aspect of urban systems and thereby encourage further developments in this field.

The dynamic urban process is indeed quite complex. It involves dynamic changes in a number of key variables such as population, capital, and labor in the urban economy, and analyzing such changes even at an aggregate level is difficult enough, as has been pointed out by Bermeister and Dobell [1970]. But a dynamic urban model, to be satisfactory, should also incorporate spatial and locational elements such as accessibility, lot size, city boundaries, etc., and modeling the spatial interaction of such variables is difficult even in a static version (Fujita [1986]). In addition,

---

The author is grateful to Richard Arnott for his helpful comments and suggestions on an earlier version of this paper.

externalities tend to arise in space (Kanemoto [1986]) and may well compound their complexities in the dynamic context. All we can hope for in the present stage, therefore, is to gain some intuition and insight into the extremely complicated process of urban growth and dynamics by looking at a relatively small number of key factors which are supposedly governing the main course of the dynamic paths of urban systems.

For this purpose, the present survey will focus on those models which provide some analytical framework for possible further elaboration and refinement to make net contributions to the existing literature on urban growth and dynamics. As a result, much of the less analytical, but often quite inspiring works will be omitted: one such example is Jacobs [1970] which stresses the importance of diversity and interaction as a source of urban growth. Unfortunately, in this survey space is too limited to include those types of studies, which might be useful in addressing a broader set of questions such as the reasons for the birth and death of a city. We will instead turn to particular models from the outset.

It may be helpful to classify various approaches to urban dynamics, which will be covered in this survey. First of all, in terms of types of dynamic analysis, we can distinguish between stability analysis and growth analysis. Dynamic stability analysis considers some adjustment mechanism to determine the dynamic paths of variables toward an equilibrium in a system with given endowments of resources and technology, whereas growth analysis investigates the dynamic motion of a growing system with its endowments of resources and possibly technology changing through time. In the present context, stability analysis concerns the dynamic adjustment process of the internal structure and configuration of the urban economy, whose overall growth performance and dynamic behavior are treated by growth analysis. We will review these two types of dynamic analysis in turn.

Furthermore, in terms of types of dynamic models, there are two kinds of dynamic urban models developed in the literature, namely, urban production models and urban residential models. The former models focus primarily on industrial production and employment in the urban economy without explicit analysis of residential activity. The latter models incorporate residential land and housing consumption explicitly and the production aspect is treated rather simply. We will first take up urban production/employment models, and then examine urban residential land/housing models. Both the stability and growth analyses of each of these types of dynamic models will be reviewed in this survey.

More specifically, in Section 2 we overview "non-spatial" dynamic urban production models which attempt to analyze the growth process of production and employment in a city or a metropolitan region. These spaceless urban models are direct applications of the aggregative analysis of economic growth and can be classified into three categories. First, "demand-oriented models" assume the demand for the city's output to be the main cause of urban growth while "supply-oriented models" focus on the supply of factors of production in the city. These two extreme views are reconciled by "demand-supply interactive models," which take full account of demand and supply in generating long-run urban growth processes.

Urban production models with explicit attention paid to both time and space are reviewed in Section 3. These spatial production models are based on the original von Thünen model of production in a monocentric region. We first survey dynamic adjustment models are based on the original von Thünen model of production in a monocentric region. We first survey dynamic adjustment economy. Then, long-run growth models which treat spatially expanding cities through time are examined, where the main dynamic forces are population growth, migration, transportation improvements, capital accumulation, etc.

In Section 4, we turn to urban residential models which take account of housing consumption, household location, and travel choice. Specifically, those dynamic models which draw heavily on the standard residential location model of the Alonso–Mills–Muth type are reviewed, where housing is identified with lot size and is instantaneously adjustable in size. First, dynamic stability analysis is taken up in the "closed city" case with a dynamic process of boundary adjustment and also in the "open city" case with a dynamic process of migration. Some instability results are found in the presence of certain types of externality. We then review long-run dynamic growth models which incorporate such dynamic factors as population growth, migration, transportation improvements, and capital accumulation, where no account is taken of the durability of housing. Some rural–urban migration models as well as optimal growth models are also surveyed in this context.

In Section 5, we cover those urban residential models which

explicitly consider the durability and adjustment costs of housing capital in the dynamic process of urban growth. In the literature on durable housing, two types of urban growth models can be distinguished according to the assumption on expectations, namely, myopic expectations models and perfect foresight models. Furthermore, some models are intended to be descriptive, where others are normative in nature. First, we look at myopic expectations models which are almost always descriptive, and then review perfect foresight models which are closely related to normative optimal-growth analysis. It turns out that these urban residential growth models with durable housing show strikingly different properties from the typical Alonso–Mills–Muth model.

Finally, concluding remarks and some suggestions for future research are given in Section 6. We will attempt to present a number of possible directions in which the existing models could be extended for the purpose of contributing to the construction of a satisfactory model of urban growth and dynamics.

2. NON-SPATIAL PRODUCTION GROWTH

Demand-oriented models

In the literature there are a number of urban production/employment growth models which are essentially spaceless. The most typical of these non-spatial production models are "demand-oriented models," as opposed to "supply-oriented models." Demand-oriented urban production growth models regard the exogenous growth of demand for the city's output as the main cause of urban growth. They can be broadly classified into two types, namely, the export base model and the income growth model.

First, the export base model assumes that export demand determines the city's total employment, and the exogenous growth of export demand causes urban economic growth. The export base model in its static version is explained in Pfouts [1960], Friedman and Alonso [1964], Czamanski [1964], and Thompson [1965], and its dynamic version is developed by Czamanski [1965], Paelinck [1970], Moody and Puffer [1970], and Harvey [1974].

A simplified version of the export base model can be expressed as

$$P = aE, \qquad a > 0, \tag{1}$$

$$E = E_1 + E_2, \tag{2}$$

$$E_2 = bP, \qquad b > 0, \tag{3}$$

where P is the city's total population, E is its total employment, E_1 is the amount of employment in the city's export sector, E_2 is the amount of employment in its non-export, local sector, and a and b are given and constant. By introducing a one-period time lag in (1) or (2), we find from (1)–(3)

$$P(t) - cP(t-1) = aE_1(t), \tag{4}$$

where $c \equiv ab$ and t stands for time period t. Assuming that export demand is growing exponentially at a constant rate:

$$E_1(t) = E_1(0)(1+g)^t, \qquad g > 0, \quad E_1(0) > 0, \tag{5}$$

then the solution to (4) is obtained as

$$P(t) = \frac{aE_1(0)}{1+g-c}(1+g)^{t+1} + Ac^t, \tag{6}$$

where A is a constant which can be determined by the initial condition $P(0)$. Thus $P(t)$ will converge to a steady growth equilibrium with the growth rate g, since the term Ac^t in (6) goes to zero as $t \to \infty$, if

$$0 < c < 1. \tag{7}$$

By introducing a more complicated time lag structure than above, Czamanski (1965) shows the property of oscillatory convergence if the same condition as (7) is met.

Second, the income growth model focuses on the growth of income and output, rather than employment *per se* in the urban economy. Bell [1967], Glickman [1971], and Hall and Licari [1974] set up metropolitan/regional income growth models which directly link output growth in the local export sector to the growth rate of GNP in the national economy. These models can therefore be regarded as a variant of the export base model.

On the other hand, Klein [1969], Moody and Puffer [1969], and Anderson [1970] develop the income growth model of the Keynesian type. A simple version of their dynamic model is written as follows:

$$Y(t) = C(t) + A(t), \tag{8}$$

$$C(t) = cY(t-1), \qquad 0 < c < 1, \tag{9}$$

where Y is income, C is consumption, and A is autonomous expenditure including exogenous investment, government spending, and exports minus imports. (8) and (9) lead to

$$Y(t) - cY(t-1) = A(t), \tag{10}$$

which has the same dynamic structure as (4) in the export base model. Thus, $Y(t)$ will converge to a steady growth equilibrium, given $0 < c < 1$, so long as $A(t)$ is growing exponentially.

As criticized by Richardson [1971, 1973], Engle [1974], Conroy [1975], and Miron [1979], the demand-oriented models in effect assume that the supply of factors of production are completely elastic, and thus tend to ignore the role of supply elements. It is clear at least from the theoretical point of view that those models which take account of the demand side only are inadequate as long-run dynamic urban models, since the availability of factors of production such as labor migration and capital inflow into the city should be an important determinant of its capacity or constraint to grow in the long run.

Supply-oriented models

Supply-oriented models assume that the supply of factors of production in the city basically determines the city's output and income, contrary to the demand-oriented models reviewed above. The city's production will grow as the supply of factors such as capital and labor increases internally and/or through the inflow of factors from outside of the city. The output demand is assumed to respond to the growth of supply automatically. Most of these supply-oriented models are neoclassical in nature and thus incorporate neoclassical production functions with emphasis on intra-urban as well as inter-urban factor movements, as in Borts and Stein [1964], Romans [1965], Siebert [1965], and Borts [1971].

Smith [1974, 1975] and Rabenau [1979] analyze the stability

property of the typical neoclassical urban growth model, which is expressed as follows:

$$Y = AK^aN^{1-a}, \qquad A>0, \quad 0<a<1, \tag{11}$$

$$\dot{K} = sY + v(r-\bar{r})K, \qquad s>0, \quad v>0, \tag{12}$$

$$\dot{N} = nN + m(w-\bar{w})N, \qquad n>0, \quad m>0, \tag{13}$$

where Y is output, K is capital, N is labor, r is the rental price of capital, w is the wage rate, and $\bar{r}$ and $\bar{w}$ are their corresponding "national" levels, which are given. The dot indicates differentiation with respect to time; $\dot{x} \equiv dx/dt$. (12) and (13) mean that the growth of a factor in the city is the sum of its internal growth and its inflow from outside, the latter being a function of its rate-of-return differentials and its stock in the city.

By defining $\hat{x} \equiv \dot{x}/x$ and $k \equiv K/N$, we find from (11)–(13)

$$\hat{K} = sAK^{a-1} + v(aAk^{a-1} - \bar{r}), \tag{14}$$

$$\hat{N} = n + m[(1-a)Ak^a - \bar{w}]. \tag{15}$$

Then,

$$\hat{k} = \hat{K} + \hat{N} = G(k), \tag{16}$$

where

$$G(k) \equiv sAk^{a-1} + v(aAk^{a-1} - \bar{r}) - n - m[(1-a)Ak^a - \bar{w}], \tag{17}$$

and

$$G'(k)<0, \quad \lim_{k\to 0} G(k) = \infty, \quad \lim_{k\to\infty} G(k) = -v\bar{r} - n + m\bar{w}, \tag{18}$$

which imply the existence, uniqueness, and global stability of a steady growth equilibrium with $k^*>0$, provided that $-v\bar{r} - n + m\bar{w} < 0$.

While most of the supply-oriented urban growth models assume constant returns to scale, there are a number of models which take account of the phenomenon of agglomeration effects. In fact, some authors consider agglomeration economies to be the most important cause of urban concentration and growth. Without agglomeration economies, no cities may exist in the first place.

The first rigorous analysis of a supply-oriented urban model with agglomeration economies is offered by Rabenau [1979]. His model has the production function

$$Y = A(N)K^a N^{1-a}, \qquad 0 < a < 1, \tag{19}$$

and

$$A(N) = N^b, \qquad 0 < 1 - a + b < 1, \tag{20}$$

where Y is output, K is capital, N is labor, and b is positive *or* negative, depending on whether there are agglomeration economies *or* diseconomies in urban production activities. In the typical neoclassical urban growth model, capital and labor will vary over time, according to (12) and (13). In the case of agglomeration economies ($b > 0$), the city will either explode without limit, or shrink to zero, depending on initial conditions. In the case of agglomeration diseconomies ($b < 0$), the city will converge to an equilibrium with constant values of K and N. Rabenau also takes up a more complicated case with both agglomeration economies and diseconomies. Specifically, he assumes that

$$A(N) = \left[\frac{N}{\bar{N}}\right]^b, \qquad b\begin{cases} > 0, & \text{for } N < \bar{N}, \\ < 0, & \text{for } N > \bar{N}. \end{cases} \tag{21}$$

This means that there are agglomeration economies for N less than $\bar{N}$, and diseconomies for N greater than $\bar{N}$. In this case it is shown that with relatively large initial values of K and N the urban economy will grow and converge to a stationary-state equilibrium.

There are some other types of supply-oriented models which can explain urban growth processes. Dendrinos [1982] assumes agglomeration economies as well as "congestion," which is incorporated in the population migration equation as

$$\dot{N} = m(w - \bar{w})N - hY^2, \qquad h > 0. \tag{22}$$

His analysis shows the possibility of oscillatory cycles around a stationary equilibrium. In Rabenau and Hanson [1979], based on Rabenau's optimal growth model [1976], public capital is introduced into an urban growth model in the form of urban infrastructure, say Z, which enters the production function as

$$Y = A(Z/N)K^a N^{1-a}, \qquad A'(\ ) > 0, \tag{23}$$

where public capital per worker Z/N gives essentially the same effect as agglomeration economies. Given that the urban government uses a payroll tax to finance its public investment projects so as to maximize the present value of the future stream of utility for its average resident, the urban economy is shown to approach a steady growth equilibrium with private capital and labor growing at a constant rate which is equal to the sum of the natural rate and the migration rate. If this long-run growth rate is positive, relatively large initial values of Z/N will ensure self-sustained urban growth.

The neoclassical model of urban growth has its own weaknesses with regard to the underlying assumptions of perfect competition, full employment, free factor mobility, etc., as pointed out by several authors such as Richardson [1971, 1973]. It is fair to say that the neoclassical approach with its exclusive emphasis on the supply side may be less appropriate for the growth analysis of an urban economy than for the national economy. In determining the dynamic processes of urban growth, the effect of supply responses to the demand side seems as important as demand responses to the supply side in the long run. This will logically lead us to the kind of dynamic urban models which can take full account of the interaction of demand and supply.

Demand–supply interactive models

In the literature, one of the earliest attempts to construct an urban growth model with both demand and supply elements is made by Niedercorn and Kain [1963] and Niedercorn [1963]. Their model is intended to be an extension of the export base type model. A simplified version of the Niedercorn–Kain model is expressed as follows. An "equilibrium" level or normal level of manufacturing employment E^e is assumed to be an increasing function of urban population P, that is,

$$E^e = aP, \qquad a > 0. \tag{24}$$

And the actual level of manufacturing employment E will change in response to the relative deviation of the actual level of employment from its equilibrium level:

$$\hat{E} = b\frac{E^e - E}{E}, \qquad b > 0. \tag{25}$$

Furthermore, the rate of change of urban population is a linear function of the rate of change of employment:

$$\hat{P} = m\hat{E} + n, \qquad m > 0, \quad n > 0. \tag{26}$$

Thus, (24)–(26) lead to

$$(P/\hat{E}) = \hat{P} - \hat{E} = -ab(1-m)(P/E) + b(1-m) + n. \tag{27}$$

This system has a unique steady growth equilibrium and is globally stable, provided that $0 < m < 1$.

On the other hand, Muth [1968, 1971, 1972] underscores the importance of both demand and supply in urban growth processes, in contrast to the export base model, and sets up the following demand–supply interactive model:

$$\hat{E} = a\hat{P} + b, \qquad a > 0, \quad b > 0, \tag{28}$$

$$\hat{P} = m\hat{E} + n, \qquad m > 0, \quad n > 0, \tag{29}$$

where employment growth $\hat{E}$ is affected by population growth $\hat{P}$, and vice versa. The system (28) and (29) can be solved for $\hat{E}$ and $\hat{P}$ as

$$\hat{E} = (an + b)/(1 - am) > 0, \tag{30}$$

$$\hat{P} = (bm + n)/(1 - am) > 0, \tag{31}$$

provided that $am < 1$. Somewhat similar models are considered by Okun [1968], Lewis and Prescott [1972], and Greenwood [1973], which also take into account the interaction of demand and supply through wage and income variables which affect population and employment growth. As criticized by Mazek and Chang [1972], the Muth model generally fails to yield a steady growth equilibrium, since $\hat{E}$ and $\hat{P}$ are not equal to each other unless $an + b = bm + n$.

There is yet another type of demand–supply interactive model, which is based on the principle of "cumulative causation." This principle, which was first suggested by Myrdal [1957], emphasizes the existence of agglomeration economies and productivity growth in manufacturing. More specifically, the model assumes that the endogenous growth of labor productivity depends on the rate of output and particularly export growth. This means that the growth of demand for output affects the supply side through productivity growth, which in turn will reduce the cost of production, leading to higher demand growth in manufacturing and exports.

According to Kaldor [1970], Richardson [1973, 1978], and Dixon and Thirlwall [1975], the cumulative causation model assumes the growth rate of labor productivity r to be a linear function of the growth rate of output g:

$$r = ag + b, \qquad a > 0, \quad b > 0, \tag{32}$$

where g is assumed to be proportional to the growth rate of export demand x,

$$g = cx, \qquad c > 0, \tag{33}$$

and x is a decreasing function of the rate of export price increase $\hat{p}$, which is equal to the rate of nominal wage increase z minus the rate of productivity growth r,

$$x = h - s\hat{p} = h - s(z - r), \qquad h > 0, \quad s > 0, \quad z > 0. \tag{34}$$

Combining (32)–(34), we find

$$g = acsg + c(h + bs - zs), \tag{35}$$

which can be solved for g as

$$g^* = c(h + bs - zs)/(1 - acs), \tag{36}$$

assuming that $acs < 1$. Furthermore, a one-period time lag is introduced into (32) so that

$$x(t) = h - s\hat{p}(t-1) = h - s[z - r(t-1)], \tag{37}$$

as in Dixon and Thirlwall. The rate of output growth in period t, $g(t)$, can generally be assumed to depend on the lagged value of itself $g(t-1)$, due to the time lag in (32), (33), or (34), as considered by Richardson. In any case, we have

$$g(t) = acsg(t-1) + c(h + bs - zs). \tag{38}$$

It is clear that this system will converge to a steady growth rate of output $g(t) = g(t-1)$, if $0 < acs < 1$ and $c(h + bs - zs) > 0$.

While the demand–supply interactive models reviewed above take account of many important dynamic factors, those models are still completely spaceless. It should be said that the dynamic process of urban growth and adjustment cannot be fully understood without explicitly analyzing spatial and locational elements. Even for the analysis of urban production growth only, it is necessary to consider the spatial patterns of production and employment as well as the location choice behavior of industries and firms explicitly.

3. SPATIAL PRODUCTION MODELS

Dynamic stability analysis

We are in a position of examining dynamic production models of the von Thünen type, which explicitly incorporate the spatial and locational aspects of economic activity. Based on the von Thünen-type monocentric model, two kinds of dynamic analyses can be carried out, namely, dynamic stability analysis and long-run growth analysis. The former is to investigate the dynamic stability property of spatial equilibrium in a static system, where the latter treats the long-run growth behavior of a dynamic system.

Let us first take up the former analysis. To see the dynamic stability property of the von Thünen model as reformulated in Beckman [1972], Solow [1973], Miyao [1977a, 1981]. It is assumed that in a homogeneous plain there are a number of industries producing different kinds of products subject to constant-returns-to-scale production functions, using land and labor as inputs. All producers in the same industry have identical production functions and identical transport cost functions, and all transport their products to the central market of the city. In equilibrium, industries are located in concentric rings, or zones, around the central market in such a way that each zone is filled exclusively with producers in a single industry. A producer in industry i ($i = 1, \ldots, m$), located at distance x from the central market, operates at the minimum cost per unit of output, $C_i[r(x), w]$, where $r(x)$ is the land rent at x and w is the wage rate. Under perfect competition, industry i's unit production cost C_i is equal to its product price p_i minus unit transport cost c_i:

$$C_i[r_i(x), w] = p_i - c_i(x) \qquad (i = 1, \ldots, m), \tag{39}$$

where p_i is exogenously given. This defines industry i's bid rent $r_i(x)$ as

$$r_i(x) = r_i[p_i - c_i(x), w] = r_i(x, w) \quad \text{for } x_{i-1} \leqq x \leqq x_i, \tag{40}$$

where industry i's bid rent becomes the prevailing market rent $r(x)$ in zone i between its inner boundary x_{i-1} and outer boundary x_i $(i=1, \ldots, m)$. Since industry i's labor–land ratio at x, $n_i(x)$, is a function of $r_i(x)$ and w, we can find from (40) that

$$n_i(x) = n_i[r_i(x, w), w] = n_i(x, w) \quad \text{for } x_{i-1} \leqq x \leqq x_i. \tag{41}$$

Assuming that labor is freely mobile within the city, the full employment condition for the city as a whole is

$$2\pi \sum_{i=1}^{m} \int_{x_{i-1}}^{x_i} g(x) n_i(x) x \, dx = N, \tag{42}$$

where N is the total population (labor force) which is a given constant, and $g(x)$ is a fraction of the land area available for industrial use at each distance x. Finally, the market rent function should be continuous, particularly at every boundary:

$$r_i(x_i) = r_{i+1}(x_i) \qquad (i=1, \ldots, m-1), \quad r_m(x_m) = r_0, \tag{43}$$

where r_0 is the opportunity cost of land, e.g., agricultural land rent, which is given exogenously. The system, (40)–(43), can determine the equilibrium values of w and x_i $(i=1, \ldots, m)$ and the equilibrium functional forms of $r_i(x)$ and $n_i(x)$ $(i=1, \ldots, m)$.

Miyao [1977a, 1981] considers two alternative processes of dynamic stability adjustment: boundary adjustment and wage adjustment. First, each boundary between two industries is assumed to adjust through time in such a way that the position of a boundary will move outward *or* inward, according to whether the bid rent of the industry located inside the boundary is higher *or* lower than that of the industry outside the boundary. This process can be formalized as

$$\begin{aligned} \dot{x}_i &= f_i[r_i(x_i, w) - r_{i+1}(x_i, w)] \qquad (i=1, \ldots, m-1), \\ \dot{x}_m &= f_m[r_m(x_m, w) - r_0], \end{aligned} \tag{44}$$

with $f_i'(\ ) > 0$ and $f_i(0) = 0$, where w is a function of x_i's $(i = 1, \ldots, m)$ from (41) and (42): $w = w(x_1, \ldots, x_m)$. Thus, the system (44) can generate a dynamic path of x_i's through time. It is shown to be locally stable for any set of positive speeds of adjustment $f_i'(0)>0$, if the well-known "von Thünen condition"

$$c_i'(x_i)/h_i(x_i) > c_{i+1}'(x_i)/h_{i+1}(x_i) \qquad (i=1, \ldots . m-1) \tag{45}$$

is satisfied at the equilibrium, where $h_i(x)$ is industry i's land-output ratio at x.

Second, the wage rate is assumed to rise *or* fall, depending on whether the excess demand for labor is positive *or* negative, whereas all the other variables are instantaneously adjusted so as to satisfy (40), (41), and (43). Define the total labor demand function

$$G(w) \equiv 2\pi \sum_{i-1}^{m} \int_{x_{i-1}}^{x_i} g(x) n_i(x, w) x \, dx, \tag{46}$$

where x_i can be expressed as a function of w by solving (43) for x_i in view of (40), and thus the total demand for labor G becomes a sole function of w. The dynamic process of wage adjustment is given as

$$\dot{w} = f[G(w) - N] \tag{47}$$

with $f'(\ )>0$ and $f(0)=0$. This process proves to be locally stable for any positive speed of adjustment $f'(0)>0$, if the von Thünen condition (45) is met. In fact it can be shown that $G'(w)<0$ in a small neighborhood of equilibrium, given (45). Note that this kind of adjustment process is also discussed in Solow [1973], where only one industry is surrounded by a homogenous group of households in a monocentric city.

Day and Tinney [1969], Day and Kennedy [1970], and Day, Kennedy, and Tinney [1978] develop a somewhat different version of the von Thünen model and examine the dynamic stability of land use patterns by applying a recursive programming method. Due to their assumption that product prices are endogenously determined and that production decisions are based on the lagged values of product prices, the model tends to exhibit a variety of long-run behavior, including a possibility of spatial mixing of multi-products in an intermediate segment of the region. This model is further modified in Okabe and Kume [1983] by deriving product demand functions from a utility function explicitly and by investigating a dynamic adjustment process analytically. It is shown that land use patterns are rather unstable and are likely to fluctuate through time. This conclusion obviously results from the assumption of myopic price expectations and the cobweb-type adjustment mechanism.

Long-run growth analysis

Next, we shall focus on long-run growth analysis and review dynamic production growth models which incorporate spatial elements explicitly. These models are essentially based on the von Thünen-type monocentric city model, and are dynamized by introducing population growth, demand growth, or transportation investment.

Miyao [1977b, 1981] presents urban production growth models with population growth and transportation improvements. His first model is a neoclassical growth model with exogenous population growth and endogenous transportation improvements. There is assumed to be only one industry having a constant-returns-to-scale production function and using land and labor as inputs. In equilibrium, unit production cost C should be equal to the "net price" of the product:

$$C[r(x), w] = 1 - \tau - cx, \tag{48}$$

where the product price is normalized as unity, τ is the rate of taxation to finance transportation investment, and c is unit transport cost. The full employment condition can be written as

$$2\pi g \int_0^{x_1} n(x)x\, dx = N, \tag{49}$$

where g is a constant fraction of land used for production, x_1 is the urban boundary, and N is total labor force in the city. Since the market rent function should be continuous,

$$r(x_1) = r_0, \tag{50}$$

where r_0 is agricultural land rent, which is exogenously given. The system can determine the equilibrium values of w and x_1 and the equilibrium functional forms of $r(x)$ and $n(x)$, given N, c, and all the other parameter values.

To dynamize the model, define

$$k \equiv 1/(Nc^2). \tag{51}$$

It can be shown that w is stationary over time if and only if k is stationary, i.e., $0 = \hat{k} = -2\hat{c} - \hat{N}$. In other words, in order to maintain a stationary value of the wage rate, the rate of population growth $\hat{N}$ must be twice as high as the rate of decrease of unit transport cost $(-\hat{c})$. N is assumed to be growing at a constant rate,

$$\hat{N} = n > 0, \tag{52}$$

and the rate of decrease of unit transport cost is an increasing function of the amount of transportation investment per unit of land devoted to transportation,

$$-\hat{c} = f(S/J) \tag{53}$$

with $f'(\ ) > 0$, $f(0) = 0$, and $f(\infty) = \infty$, where S is total transportation investment which is equal to total tax revenue, and J is the land area used for transportation and is a constant fraction of land at each distance from the center. Since S/J can be expressed as a sole function of k, we find the fundamental dynamic equation,

$$\hat{k} = -2\hat{c} - \hat{N} = 2f(S/J) - n = H(k) - n. \tag{54}$$

The existence, uniqueness, and global stability of a steady growth equilibrium with $\hat{k} = 0$ can be established, if the production function is Cobb–Douglas and the agricultural land rent is zero. In this case, defining total net output as total gross output minus total tax payment and total transport cost, we can show that the steady growth equilibrium value of net output per capita is maximized when the tax rate is equal to the land elasticity of output, that is, the ratio of total land rent to total net output. This result is analogous to the golden rule of capital accumulation in the neoclassical theory of economic growth.

Miyao's second model [1981] treats exogenous transportation improvements and endogenous population growth. Unit transport cost is assumed to be decreasing at an exogenously given rate,

$$-\hat{c} = b > 0, \tag{55}$$

while the rate of net inflow of population to the city depends on the difference between the wage rate in the city w and the national wage rate $\bar{w}$, which is given exogenously,

$$\hat{N} = n(w - \bar{w}), \tag{56}$$

where $n'(\ ) > 0$, $n(0) = 0$, and $n(\infty) = \infty$. Since w is shown to be a sole function of k, the fundamental dynamic equation becomes

$$\hat{k} = -2\hat{c} - \hat{N} = 2b - n[w(k) - \bar{w}]. \tag{57}$$

The right-hand side of (57) is decreasing in k under some mild assumptions on the production function and, therefore, the existence, uniqueness, and global stability of a steady growth equilibrium can be readily established.

Carlberg [1981] introduces capital into a von Thünen-type growth model. He shows that if the amount of land is exogenously fixed and population is growing at a positive constant rate, then the Cobb–Douglas production function is the only CES case where long-run growth is possible. Of course, in this instance, population density will increase over time. Moreover, it is proved that if the urban boundary is determined endogenously as in the Miyao models, long-run steady growth may not be possible even in the Cobb–Douglas case. The main difference between Carlberg's results and Miyao's is due to the fact that Carlberg does not assume a steady improvement in transportation over time.

The spatial production models reviewed above are neoclassical in nature and thus essentially supply-oriented. In the literature there are some other kinds of spatial production growth models, which may be regarded as demand-supply interactive. One such model is the econometric model of Eagle, Fisher, Harris, and Rothenberg [1972] which deals with various aspects of metropolitan growth including production, housing, government, etc. A submodel of the whole system is explained in Engle [1974], where the dynamics of the "Macro subsystem" is represented by the following equations:

$$\hat{W} = F(u, q^e), \qquad F_1 < 0, \quad F_2 > 0, \tag{58}$$

$$\hat{K} = G(v), \qquad G' > 0, \tag{59}$$

$$\hat{M} = H(w, u), \qquad H_1 > 0, \quad H_2 < 0, \tag{60}$$

where W is the nominal wage rate, K is capital, M is population, u is the unemployment rate, q^e is the expected rate of inflation, v is the rate of return on capital, and w is the real wage rate. These variables are defined for the urban economy in question, while the corresponding "national" values are assumed to be given and constant.

Based on Engle's model, Miyao [1980, 1981] offers a von Thünen-type dynamic production model and investigates the dynamic property of the model rigorously. In his model, a firm located at distance x from the central market has the Cobb–Douglas production function,

$$Y(x) = L(x)^a K(x)^b N(x)^c, \quad a, b, c > 0, \quad a + b + c = 1, \tag{61}$$

where $Y(x)$, $L(x)$, $K(x)$, and $N(x)$ are the firm's output, land, capital, and labor, respectively, at distance x. Assuming that unit transport cost is constant and the opportunity cost of land is zero, the following aggregate production function for the urban area as a whole can be obtained,

$$Y = Ap^{2a}K^b N^c, \qquad A > 0, \tag{62}$$

where Y, K, and N are the aggregate amounts of output, capital, and labor, respectively, and p is the price of output. It is further assumed that the total demand for output is

$$D = Bp^{-s}e^{ht}, \qquad B, s, h > 0, \tag{63}$$

which yields

$$\hat{D} = h - s\hat{p}. \tag{64}$$

In a steady growth equilibrium, Y should equal D, and all the factors must grow at the same rate as Y and D. This means that

$$h - s\hat{p} = \hat{L} = 2\hat{p}, \tag{65}$$

$$h - s\hat{p} = \hat{K} = G(v), \tag{66}$$

$$h - s\hat{P} = \hat{N} = \hat{M} = H(w, u), \tag{67}$$

$$\hat{p} = \hat{W} = F(u, \hat{p}), \tag{68}$$

where it is assumed that the expected rate of inflation q^e is equal to the actual rate $\hat{p}$. Note that the system, as described by (65)–(68), can determine the steady growth equilibrium values of $\hat{p}$, v, w, and u. The equilibrium is shown to be locally stable if

$$F_2 < 1 + (2a/c) + [(a + b)s/c] \tag{69}$$

is satisfied. While local stability is obtained under this condition, global stability cannot be ensured in general and the system tends to exhibit a variety of dynamic behavior including cyclical fluctuations over time.

It should be pointed out that there are two major weaknesses in almost all the dynamic urban production models reviewed so far. The first is the lack of analysis of interaction between production and residential activities in the city. In fact, there are very few urban models, whether dynamic or static, which take account of both industry and housing in a spatial setting in the literature. Needless to say, it is important to analyze spatial interaction and land allocation between industries and firms on one hand and consumers and workers on the other. Another weakness is the neglect of the durability of structure and capital in the dynamic process of production growth. Correspondingly, producers' expectations about future price/quantity variables are very naively treated by essentially assuming static or myopic expectations. Some of these weaknesses are being remedied in dynamic models of residential growth, which we will survey next.

4. NEOCLASSICAL RESIDENTIAL MODELS

Dynamic stability analysis

Let us examine the dynamics of urban residential models originally developed by Alonso [1964], Mills [1967], Muth [1969], and others. These models may be called "neoclassical" in the sense that the main focus is on the long-run equilibrium patterns of residential location and urban structure and the durability of housing capital is largely ignored. First, we shall review the static version of the Alonso–Mills–Muth model and then investigate the dynamic stability property of the equilibrium in the model.

Consider a monocentric city with many household classes. There are assumed to be n household classes with different utility functions, different income levels, and/or different transport cost functions, whereas each class consists of homogeneous households with identical utility, income, and transport cost functions. Just as in the monocentric production model reviewed in the previous section, households are located in concentric rings (zones) around the central business district (CBD). Both zones and classes are numbered in such a way that zone i corresponds to class i. A household in class i, located at distance x from the CBD, maximizes its utility, which depends on a consumption good z_i and residential land space h_i, that is, $U_i(x) = U_i[z_i(x), h_i(x)]$, subject to the budget constraint, $z_i(x) + r(x)h_i(x) = w_i - c_i(x)$. In this approach, the price of the consumption good is exogenously given and normalized as unity, $r(x)$ is the market land rent at x, w_i is income for class i, and $c_i(x)$ is transport (commuting) cost for class i at x. In terms of the indirect utility function, we find

$$V_i[r_i(x), w_i - c_i(x)] = u_i \qquad (i = 1, \ldots, n), \tag{70}$$

where u_i is the utility level which all households in class i must achieve regardless of their locations, and $r_i(x)$ is class i's bid rent, that is, the maximum rent that households in class i are willing to pay for each location x. Class i's bid rent is obtained by solving (70) for $r_i(x)$ as

$$r_i(x) = r_i[w_i - c_i(x), u_i] \quad \text{for } x_{i-1} \leqq x \leqq x_i, \tag{71}$$

and the demand for land by a household in class i at x becomes

$$h_i(x) = h_i[r_i(x), u_i] = h_i[w_i - c_i(x), u_i] \quad \text{for } x_{i-1} \leqq x \leqq x_i, \tag{72}$$

where x_{i-1} and x_i are the inner and outer boundaries of zone i, respectively. The condition that all households in class i should reside in zone i may be written as

$$2\pi \int_{x_{i-1}}^{x_i} \frac{g(x)x}{h_i(x)}\, dx = N_i \qquad (i = 1, \ldots, m), \tag{73}$$

where N_i is the total number of households in class i, and $g(x)$ is a fraction of land available for housing at each x. Finally, the condition that the market rent should be continuous at all boundaries is

$$r_i(x_i) = r_{i+1}(x_i) \quad (i = 1, \ldots, m-1), \qquad r_m(x_m) = r_0, \tag{74}$$

where r_0 is the opportunity cost of land which is given exogenously.

As Wheaton [1974] points out, we can distinguish between the "closed city" case and the "open city" case. In the closed city case, the total number of households in each class, N_i $(i = 1, \ldots, m)$, is exogenously given, while the utility level for each class, u_i $(i = 1, \ldots, m)$, is endogenously determined within the system (71)–(74). In the open city case, on the other hand, the utility levels are exogenous and the numbers of households are endogenous, just contrary to the closed city case. Wheaton [1974], Miyao [1975, 1981], and Hartwick, Schweizer, and Varaiya [1976a, 1976b] obtain some comparative static results in the closed city case and show that the city tends to expand outward, as N_i increases, w_i increases, or r_0 decreases. These authors also prove that a decrease in unit transport cost has qualitatively the same effect as an increase in the wage rate and flattens the rent gradient. The comparative static analysis of the open city is conducted in Wheaton [1974] and Miyao [1979, 1981], which show that rents will increase at all locations and the city will expand, as income rises, unit transport cost falls, the level of utility falls, or the opportunity cost of land falls. In contrast to the closed city, there is no flattening of the rent gradient when income increases or unit transport cost decreases in the open city. As shown by Miyao in the open city with m household classes, changes in w_i, c_i, or u_i will only affect the bid rents of class i and the inner and outer boundaries of zone i, but not the bid rents of any other class or the position of any other boundary.

The dynamic stability property of the closed city model is investigated in Miyao [1975, 1981], which introduces a dynamic adjustment process of boundary positions. More specifically, a boundary between two classes is assumed to move gradually through time in such a way as to expand outward *or* shrink inward, according to whether the bid rent of the inner class is higher *or* lower than that of the outer class at the boundary. This adjustment process can thus be expressed as

$$\begin{aligned} \dot{x}_i &= f_i[r_i(x_i) - r_{i+1}(x_i)] \qquad (i = 1, \ldots, m-1), \\ \dot{x}_m &= f_m[r_m(x_m) - r_0], \end{aligned} \tag{75}$$

where $f_i'(\ ) > 0$ and $f_i(0) = 0$. Noting that $r_i(x)$ is a function of u_i from (71) and u_i is a function of x_{i-1} and x_i from (72) and (73), we have a simultaneous differential equation system involving x_i's in (75). Just as Miyao's stability analysis of the von Thünen production model, it is shown that the system (75) is locally stable for any set of positive speeds of adjustment $f_i'(0) > 0$, provided that at each boundary the inner class has a higher ratio of marginal transport cost to land per household than the outer class,

$$c_i'(x_i)/h_i(x_i) > c_{i+1}'(x_i)/h_{i+1}(x_i) \qquad (i = 1, \ldots, m-1), \tag{76}$$

and land is a non-Giffen good at each location,

$$\partial h_i(x)/\partial r_i(x) < 0 \qquad (i = 1, \ldots, m), \tag{77}$$

where h_i is the Marshallian demand function for land, and all the variables are evaluated at the equilibrium.

With regard to the open city case, Miyao [1979, 1981] conducts a dynamic stability analysis by introducing an adjustment process of household movement into and out of the city through time. The number of households in each class N_i is assumed to increase due to in-migration *or* decrease due to out-migration, as the utility level u_i achieved by the households in class i in the city is higher *or* lower than a certain utility level $\bar{u}_i$ which those households can attain outside the city,

$$\dot{N}_i = f_i(u_i - \bar{u}_i) \qquad (i = 1, \ldots, m), \tag{78}$$

with $f_i'(\ ) > 0$ and $f_i(0) = 0$, where u_i is a function of N_i's at each point in time, as in the closed city case. The long-run equilibrium condition that $\dot{N}_i = 0$ will give the equilibrium values of N_i's in the open city case. The system (78) can then be shown to be locally stable for any positive speeds of adjustment $f_i'(0) > 0$, if both (76) and (77) are satisfied.

In the model above, there is assumed to be no externality affecting any household. If, however, certain types of externality among households, the equilibrium may become unstable in the open city case. Following Schelling's dynamic, but non-spatial models [1969, 1971], Miyao [1978, 1981] introduces negative inter-group externality, which means that different classes of households dislike each other. In the case of two household classes having different income levels with Cobb–Douglas utility functions

$$U_i = z_i^a h_i^b N_j^{-c_i}, \qquad i \neq j \ (i, j = 1, 2) \tag{79}$$

with a, b, and c_i being positive constants, the "interior" equilibrium with $N_1 > 0$ and $N_2 > 0$ is shown to be unstable, provided that the degree of negative externality is so high that $c_i \geqq b$ $(i = 1, 2)$, even if both (76) and (77) are met. Kanemoto [1980a, 1980b] and Miyao, Shapiro, and Knapp [1980] also obtain instability results in their dynamic models with somewhat different types of negative externality. It should be noted that the Miyao–Shapiro–Knapp model is one of the few which offer a dynamic analysis in the urban economy with both production and residential activities explicitly incorporated.

Urban residential growth

We are now in a position of reviewing long-run residential growth models which are based on the neoclassical residential model of the Alonso–Mills–Muth type. Here, the dynamic factors are population growth, transportation improvements, income growth, etc., and the long-run dynamic behavior of the growing residential city is examined by utilizing the method of economic growth analysis.

Miyao [1977c, 1981] assumes exogenous population growth and endogenous transportation improvements in a typical monocentric city model with one homogenous class of households. The utility function is Cobb–Douglas,

$$U(x) = z(x)^a h(x)^b, \qquad a, b > 0, \tag{80}$$

which is maximized, subject to

$$z(x) + r(x)h(x) = 1 - \tau - cx, \tag{81}$$

where the price of the consumption good and household income are both normalized as unity, τ is the tax rate, and c is unit transport cost. Then the bid rent function and the land demand function become

$$r(x) = A(1 - \tau - cx)^{(a+b)}u^{-1/b}, \tag{82}$$

$$h(x) = B(1 - \tau - cx)^{-a/b}u^{-1/b}, \tag{83}$$

respectively, where A and B are some positive constants, and u is the maximized level of utility. The condition that all households must be housed in the city can be written as

$$2\pi g \int_0^{x_1} [x/h(x)]\, dx = Cu^{-1/b} \int_0^{x_1} x(1 - \tau - cx)^{a/b}\, dx = N, \tag{84}$$

where g is a constant fraction of land available for housing at each x, x_1 is the urban boundary, N is the total number of households in the city, and C is a positive constant. The market rent function should be continuous at x_1,

$$r(x_1) = A(1 - \tau - cx_1)^{(a+b)/b}u^{-1/b} = r_0. \tag{85}$$

To show the existence, uniqueness, and global stability of a steady growth equilibrium, it is assumed that $r_0 = 0$, which yields

$x_1 = (1 - \tau)/c$, and together with (84) leads to

$$u = Dk^b(1 - \tau)^{(a+2b)}, \tag{86}$$

where D is a positive constant, and

$$k \equiv 1/(Nc^2). \tag{87}$$

Given a constant value of τ, u is stationary if and only if k is stationary through time, that is, $0 = \hat{k} = -2\hat{c} - \hat{N}$. Here, the total urban population N is assumed to be growing at a constant rate,

$$\hat{N} = n > 0, \tag{88}$$

and the rate of decrease of unit transport cost depends on the amount of transportation investment per unit of land available for transportation,

$$-\hat{c} = f(S/J) \tag{89}$$

with $f'(\ ) > 0$, $f(0) = 0$, and $f(\infty) = \infty$, where S is total transportation investment which is equal to total tax revenue τN, and J is a constant fraction, say α, of the total land area of the city, $J = \alpha\pi(x_1)^2$. The fundamental dynamic equation becomes

$$\hat{k} = -2\hat{c} - \hat{N} = 2f[\tau N/\{\alpha\pi(x_1)^2\}] - n = 2f[\tau/\{\alpha\pi(1 - \tau)^2 k\}] - n. \tag{90}$$

Setting $\hat{k} = 0$ gives a steady growth equilibrium value of k, and the uniqueness and global stability of the equilibrium follow from (90) in the same way as in the one-sector neoclassical model of economic growth of the Solow type. It is clear from (82) and (83) that in the steady growth equilibrium both rents $r(x)$ and residential densities $1/h(x)$ will become higher at all locations and their gradients become flatter through time. As in Miyao's production model with exogenous population growth, the steady growth equilibrium level of utility is maximized when the tax rate is equal to the ratio of land rent to total net income, a result which is analogous to the golden rule of capital accumulation. Essentially the same results hold in the case of two income classes with identical Cobb–Douglas utility functions.

While the above model with exogenous population growth is based on the closed city model, a long-run growth analysis of the open city model with endogenous population growth through migration is also presented in the literature. Following Casetti [1980], Papageorgiou [1980] develops a two-sector model with rural and urban areas where production as well as residential activities take place in the open city with one household class. In the urban sector, production is assumed to exhibit increasing returns such that the wage rate w is increasing with the urban population N_u for relatively small values of N_u, but decreasing returns such that w is inversely related to N_u for larger values of N_u. Given this property, the utility level in the city is likely to be highly non-linear with respect to N_u, and increasing with N_u for some intermediate range of N_u. On the other hand, the utility level in the rural sector is assumed to be negatively related to the rural population N_r, where the total population $N = N_u + N_r$ in the economy is constant. Then, there may exist multiple equilibria where the utility levels in the two sectors are equal so that no further migration between rural and urban areas takes place. Assuming income growth because of technological progress, Papageorgiou shows that the urban population initially at the lowest equilibrium point can achieve a sudden, explosive increase toward a higher equilibrium point, when income rises sufficiently. This kind of "catastrophic" change in the urban economy also observed in Kanemoto (1980a, 1980b) under somewhat different circumstances.

By constructing a two-sector model similar to Papageorgiou's, but a little more spatially aggregated than his model, Miyao [1983] considers the natural growth of population and the dynamic adjustment of the urban boundary in addition to migration between the urban and rural sectors. The model consists of the following three dynamic equations:

$$\hat{N}_u = m(u-v)/N_r/N_u + n_u(u), \qquad m'(\ )>0, \quad n_u'(\ )>0, \tag{91}$$

$$\hat{N}_r = -m(u-v) + n_r(v), \quad n_r'(\ )>0, \tag{92}$$

$$\hat{L}_u = f(r_u - r_r), \quad f'(\ )>0, \tag{93}$$

where m, u, v, n_u, n_r, L_u, r_u, and r_r denote the rate of rural–urban migration in proportion to the rural population, the utility level in the urban sector, the utility level in the rural sector, the natural growth rate of the urban population, that of the rural population, the total amount of urban land, the urban land rent, and the rural land rent, respectively. By using the indirect utility function concept, u can be expressed as a function of the urban land rent r_u and household income in the urban sector I_u, where r_u is shown to depend on I_u and N_u/L_u. I_u is in turn assumed to be an increasing function of N_u/L_u, because of agglomeration economies in the urban sector, and thus u may be regarded as a sole function of N_u/L_u. Similarly, v can be expressed as a sole function of N_r/L_r, where L_r is the total amount of rural land, and due to the law of diminishing returns in agriculture, household income in the rural sector I_r is assumed to be a decreasing function of N_r/L_r. Supposing that the total amount of land in the economy L is fixed exogenously so that $L = L_u + L_r$, we have a complete system of differential equations (91)–(93) determining dynamic paths of N_u, N_r, and L_u through time. Specifically, Miyao analyzes two cases, that is, the case of no adjustment of boundary between the two sectors and the case of no natural population growth. In the case of no boundary adjustment with an initial value of N_u being sufficiently small, both the urban and the rural sectors will initially grow in terms of population, and then the rural population will start to decline while the urban population will continue to grow. Eventually, both sectors will start to lose population. On the other hand, in the case of no natural growth the city tends to exhibit a cyclical movement in terms of population and land, provided that the degree of urban agglomeration economies is sufficiently high. If the degree of urban agglomeration economies is relatively low, the urban population and the urban land area will monotonically approach their long-run equilibrium values.

In the literature on the neoclassical theory of urban residential growth, there are very few attempts to apply the method of optimal control analysis. On such attempt is made by Kanemoto [1980b], based on the optimality analysis of Isard and Kanemoto [1976]. Kanemoto examines the optimal growth process of a system of identical cities with both production and residential activities. As in the typical residential city model of the neoclassical type, the household utility depends on a consumption good and residential space, and transport cost is a function of distance only. In each city, production is subject to increasing returns with respect to population so that per capita output can be written as a function of the capital–labor ratio k and the total population in this city N, that is, $f(k, N)$ with $f_k > 0$ and $f_N > 0$. The total population in the system of cities as a whole is

$$M = mN, \tag{94}$$

where m is the total number of cities in the system, and M is growing at a constant rate $\hat{M} = n$. Kanemoto's optimization problem is to maximize the undiscounted sum of household utility u (minus the optimal steady-state utility level u^*) over an infinite time horizon, where households and capital are assumed to be freely mobile between cities, given a certain initial value of $k(0) = k_0$. The first stage of optimization is to choose the amount of the consumption good c and residential space for each household, given c and N, where

$$c = f(k, N) - \dot{k} - \lambda k, \tag{95}$$

λ being the rate of capital depreciation. This gives the utility level u as a function of c and N at each t, that is, $u(t) = u[c(t), N(t)]$. Then the second stage of optimization is to maximize

$$\int_0^\infty \{U[c(t), N(t)] - u^*)\, dt, \tag{96}$$

subject to (94) and (95) with $k(0) = k_0$. It is shown that along the steady-state growth path, the number of cities is increasing at the same rate as overall population growth, while leaving the configuration of each city unchanged through time, and that the optimal path which solves the above problem must converge to the steady state.

5. HOUSING DURABILITY AND EXPECTATIONS

Myopic expectations models

In the literature on housing, the importance of durability is pointed out by many authors including Muth [1973] and Evans [1975]. In particular, housing durability is regarded by Harrison and Kain [1974] as the main factor which can explain much of the cumulative growth process of American cities in the last several decades. Along the line of these studies, a number of dynamic residential models with durable housing are constructed and analyzed. It turns out that those durable housing models show strikingly different properties from the neoclassical residential model of the Alonso–Mills–Muth type. Furthermore, we can distinguish between two kinds of assumptions on expectations in those durable housing models: namely, myopic expectations and perfect foresight. First, we will survey dynamic models of durable housing with myopic expectations and later take up those models with perfect foresight.

The first complete growth model with durable housing and myopic expectations is set up in Anas [1976, 1978]. Specifically, Anas supposes that housing is perfectly durable physically, and the cost of housing demolition is so high that no replacement of existing housing can take place economically. All agents in the economy, i.e., developers, landowners, and households, have myopic expectations in the sense that they expect current variables to remain unchanged indefinitely in the future. Under these assumptions, the city experiences a sequence of new housing developments through time, with new construction taking place only at the urban fringe to accommodate its growing population. Thus, at time t the city consists of t rings of housing with the urban boundary x_t, where inside the city the ith ring "was" developed at time i with its outer boundary x_i $(i = 1, \dots, t-1)$. There is assumed to be only one homogenous class of households which maximize their utility

$$U(x)_t = [z(x)_t]^a[h(x)_t]^b, \qquad a, b > 0, \quad a + b = 1, \tag{97}$$

subject to

$$z(x)_t + p(x)_t h(x)_t - c(x)_t = w_t, \quad \text{for } 0 < x \leqq x_t, \tag{98}$$

where $z(x)_t$ and $h(x)_t$ are the amounts of a consumption good and housing, respectively, at distance x from the CBD at time t, $p(x)_t$ and $c(x)_t$ are the price of housing and transport (commuting) cost, respectively, at distance x at time t, and w_t is household income at time t. Because of the assumption of perfectly durable housing, we have $h(x)_t = h(x)_i$ for $x_{i-1} < x \leqq x_i$ $(i = 1, \dots, t-1)$. In equilibrium, the housing price gradient is negative within ring t,

$$\partial p(x)_t/\partial x = -c'(x)_t/h(x)_t < 0 \quad \text{for } x_{t-1} < x \leqq x_t, \tag{99}$$

and the maximized utility level at time t, u_t^*, is common for all households at all locations within the city,

$$U(x)_t = u_t^* \quad \text{for } x_{i-1} < x \leqq x_i \quad (i = 1, \dots, t), \tag{100}$$

since all households are freely mobile with no moving cost incurred within the city. Housing is supplied competitively by developers who bid up land rents so as to maximize

$$r(x)_t = [p(x)_t h(x)_t - \rho_t K(x)_t - \omega_t N(x)_t]/L(x)_t \quad \text{for } 0 < x \leqq x_t, \tag{101}$$

with respect to capital $K(x)_t$, labor $N(x)_t$, and land $L(x)_t$, subject to

$$h(x)_t = [K(x)_t]^\alpha [L(x)_t]^\beta [N(x)_t]^\gamma, \quad \alpha + \beta + \gamma = 1, \quad \text{for} \quad 0 < x \leqq x_t, \tag{102}$$

where $r(x)_t$ is the land rent at distance x at time t, and ρ_t and ω_t are the prices of capital and labor, respectively, at time t. Since the production function exhibits constant returns to scale, there is no profit in housing production in the equilibrium. Furthermore, the additional number of households $M_t - M_{t-1}$ must be accommodated in ring t,

$$M_t - M_{t-1} = 2\pi \int_{x_{t-1}}^{x_t} [x/L(x)_t]\, dx, \tag{103}$$

and the market rent function should be continuous at x_t,

$$r(x_t)_t = r_{0t}, \tag{104}$$

where r_{0t} is the opportunity cost of land at time t.

First, Anas [1978] examines the closed city case. Combining $p(x)_t h(x)_t = b[w_t - c(x)_t]$ from (97) and (98) and $r(x)_t L(x)_t = \beta p(x)_t h(x)_t$ from (102), and also considering (104), we find

$$1/L(x_t)_t = r_{0t}/[\beta b\{w_t - c(x_t)_t\}]. \tag{105}$$

This implies that the sequence of boundary densities, $1/L(x_1)_1, \ldots, 1/L(x_t)_t$, is increasing with distance, and will be increasing faster, as r_{0t} is rising, w_t is falling, or c_t is rising through time, where c_t is unit transport cost. It also follows that sufficiently increasing income and/or decreasing unit transport cost can yield a declining sequence of boundary densities and, as a consequence, the gradient of boundary densities becomes steeper with a higher rate of income increase or transport cost decrease. All these properties contrast sharply with those of the Alonso–Mills–Muth model. On the other hand, in the open city case with u_t^* being an exogenous parameter, the maximization problem (101) gives

$$1/L(x_t)_t = C(u_t^*)^{-1}(r_{0t})^{(1-\beta b)}(\rho_t)^{-\alpha b}(\omega_t)^{-\gamma b}, \qquad (106)$$

where C is a positive constant. This means that increases in r_{0t} or decreases in u_t^* will lead to increasing boundary densities, *provided that* the urban boundary is expanding through time. Contrary to the closed city case, boundary densities will be affected by changes in ρ_t and ω_t, but not by changes in w_t or c_t. It is further shown that in both the open city and the closed city cases with rising income and rising utility, the land price and rent at any given x will first increase through time and subsequently decline if utility increases sufficiently. As a result, land prices and rents tend to rise initially in the inner segment of the city, and then will fall, leading to a negative rent gradient for the inner segment and eventually negative rent levels at some locations.

In his vintage model of residential growth, Brueckner [1980a] assumes that demolition is costless, while keeping the assumption of myopic expectations. His model supposes that housing services are produced according to the constant-returns-to-scale production function $h(x)_t = F[K(x)_t, L(x)_t]$ at distance x from the CBD at time t, using capital K and land L as inputs. Housing is assumed to be deteriorating physically at a constant rate λ, so that the amount of housing services offered at time t' by a house built at time t is $h(x)_t e^{-\lambda(t'-t)}$. Since production is subject to constant returns to scale, the zero profit condition can be written as

$$[p(x)_t/(\lambda+\theta)]f[k(x)_t] - V_t k(x)_t = \Pi(x)_t, \qquad (107)$$

where $h/L = F(K/L, 1) \equiv f(k)$, $p(x)_t$ is the price of housing services, θ is the interest rate, V_t is the price of capital, and $\Pi(x)_t$ is the price of land. A condition under which housing redevelopment occurs is derived by comparing the expected profit from continuing to operate an existing building with the expected profit from demolishing the existing building and constructing a new one on the original land. Then it follows that redevelopment occurs if the present value of the expected revenue from redevelopment, net of new development cost, at time t,

$$[p(x)_t^i/(\lambda+\theta)]f[k(x)_t] - V_t k(x)_t \qquad (108)$$

is greater than the present value of the expected revenue from continuing to operate an old house built at time i per unit of land from time t on, i.e.,

$$[p(x)_t^i/(\lambda + \theta)]f[k(x)_i]e^{-\lambda(t-i)}, \tag{109}$$

where $p(x)_t^i$ is the price of housing services offered at time t by a house built at time i. Noting that (108) is equal to the left-hand side of (107), we can restate the condition for redevelopment as follows: redevelopment takes place if the present value of the expected revenue from continuing to utilize an old building falls below the price of the original land. In this model with the assumption of zero demolition cost, unlike the Anas model, land rents will never become negative, as redevelopment becomes profitable before land rents fall below zero. In fact, Brueckner's numerical simulation in his open city model with one homogeneous class of households suggests that there seems to be a strong tendency toward redevelopment in the inner segment of the city, and, as a result, building ages tend to increase discontinuously with distance, leading to discontinuous decreases in structural and population densities with distance.

Following Anas and Brueckner, Wheaton [1982a, 1983] presents a myopic expectations model in the closed city case with a homogeneous class of households having a utility function which directly depends on the amounts of housing capital and residential land. His closed city analysis shows that redevelopment tends to yield substantially higher structural and population densities than those in the old surrounding areas, just as Brueckner's open city analysis shows. Furthermore, Wheaton's simulation results indicate generally declining, but often discontinuous density functions with distance. It is also pointed out that population growth leads to redevelopment because existing population density becomes suboptimal, and rising income tends to make the amount of capital in existing housing suboptimal and thus cause redevelopment in the closed city.

The Anas–Brueckner–Wheaton model with one household class is extended by Brueckner [1980b] and Vousden [1980] so as to follow two household classes with different income levels, but with identical utility functions in the open city case. Brueckner proves that initially the household class with the higher ratio of income to unit transport cost lives in the outer segment of the city and the process of filtering takes place around the boundary between the two classes. His simulation results show that filtering tends to delay redevelopment around the boundary and, as a result, redevelopment initially occurs in the inner segment of the city as well as in some part of the outer segment except the blocks of housing which underwent filtering around the boundary. This produces irregular and discontinuous density patterns with a sudden jump in density in the outer segment of the city. Eventually, the interaction of redevelopment and filtering yields spatial intermixing and leapfrogging in terms of household income, density, and building age structure. This tendency toward the spatial intermixing of two income classes, especially in the outer segment of the city, is also pointed out in Vousden [1980], even though filtering may not occur in the case of constant utility through time. All these results are quite different from the patterns of complete segregation and uniformly declining density found in the Alonso–Mills–Muth model with many household classes.

Perfect foresight models

It might be argued that the assumption of myopic expectations is quite unrealistic in the context of urban growth, since anticipated changes such as accelerated changes in population and property values in the future often seems to play a crucial role in housing development and land transactions in reality. As an alternative to the myopic expectations assumption, therefore, perfect foresight is assumed in several urban growth models with durable housing. It turns out that these perfect foresight models share many properties with the myopic expectations models reviewed above, but also have distinctly different properties including certain optimality results which are not obtained from the myopic expectations analysis.

There exist various kinds of perfect foresight models with durable housing in the literature. One of the pioneering works of this type is Arnott [1980], which assumes flexible dwelling unit size (in contrast to the Anas model with fixed dwelling size) with no possibility of structural depreciation or upgrading in the closed city case. On the other hand, Brueckner [1981] takes account of housing demolition and redevelopment under stationary conditions in an open city case, where dwellings are affected by depreciation and maintenance, and structural modification of dwelling units is possible only through demolition and redevelopment. Some features of these two models are adopted in the closed city model of Brueckner and Rabenau [1981] which investigates the effect of an exogenous population change that is fully anticipated by developers, and generates a variety of possible land use patterns such as leap-frog sprawl and discontinuous density gradients. These descriptive urban growth models with perfect foresight on the part of developers are further refined in Fujita [1982], which shows the possibility of positive density and rent gradients. Moreover, Wheaton [1982b, 1983] proves the possibility of a "reversed" development pattern with urban land development taking place from the urban fringe toward the center, a result which contrasts most sharply with the properties of the neoclassical urban growth models as well as the myopic expectations models reviewed above.

To see how this reversed pattern of urban development can possibly occur, consider a simplified version of the Fujita–Wheaton model with a constant unit transport cost. Following Wheaton, assume a homogeneous class of households maximizing the utility function

$$U(x)_t = U[z(x)_t, L(x)_t, K(x)_t], \tag{110}$$

subject to $z(x)_t + R(x)_t + cx = w_t$, where utility depends on a consumption good z, land L, and housing capital K, and R is the total rent for housing which is a combination of L and K at location x. Solving (110) for z and setting $U(x)_t = u_t$, we find

$$\begin{aligned} R(x)_t &= w_t - cx - z[u_t, L(x)_t, K(x)_t] \\ &= R[w_t, x, u_t, L(x)_t, K(x)_t]. \end{aligned} \tag{111}$$

Given that the ith period begins at T_{i-1} and ends at T_i ($i = 1, \ldots, n$), a developer who intends to develop a unit of land at the beginning of period t will choose L and K so as to maximize the present value of the net revenue per unit of land, $P(x; t)$, at each location x, that is,

$$\operatorname*{Max}_{L,K} P(x; t) = \sum_{i=1}^{t-1} D_i r_{0i} + \sum_{i=t}^{n} D_i \frac{R(w_i, x, u_i, L, K)}{L} - \frac{V_t K e^{-\theta T_{t-1}}}{L}, \tag{112}$$

where r_0 is the opportunity cost of land, V is the cost of housing capital, θ is the rate of interest, and D_i is the discount factor: $D_i \equiv (e^{-\theta T_{i-1}} - e^{-\theta T_i})/\theta$ for $i = 1, \ldots, n$. Furthermore, land is developed in the time period with the highest present value $P(x; i)$ at location x, and the set of locations χ_t to be developed in period t can be expressed as

$$\chi_t = \{x : P(x; t) \geqq P(x; i) \text{ for all } i\} \qquad (t = 1, \ldots, n). \quad (113)$$

Finally, the total amount of land developed in period t should be just sufficient to accommodate the population growth during the period,

$$M_t - M_{t-1} = 2\pi \int_{\chi_t} \frac{x}{L(x)_t}\, dx \qquad (t = 1, \ldots, n). \quad (114)$$

Urban land development occurs from the outside in, if the "present value bid function" $P(x; t)$ becomes steeper over time, i.e.,

$$0 > \partial P(x; t)/\partial x > \partial P(x; t+1)/\partial x, \quad (115)$$

so that $P(x; t) < P(x; t+1)$ in the inner segment of the city and $P(x; t) > P(x; t+1)$ in the outer segment. Since

$$\frac{\partial P(x; t)}{\partial x} - \frac{\partial P(x; t+1)}{\partial x} = \left[\sum_{\tau=t+1}^{n} \frac{D_i c}{L_t}\right]\left[\frac{L_t}{L_{t+1}} - e^{\theta(T_t - T_{t-1})}\right], \quad (116)$$

the inequality in (115) holds if θ is sufficiently small and L_t/L_{t+1} is greater than one and sufficiently large. The latter condition means that the density of residential development $1/L_i$ is increasing sufficiently through time, and thus some inner segment of the city is initially left vacant for higher-density development in a later period.

In a somewhat different open city model with only two time periods, Mills [1981] shows that leap-frog development and discontinuous rent gradients may occur in the case of perfect foresight and that the assumption of uncertainty and heterogeneous expectations can yield a spatial intermixing of various kinds of land use and possibly non-use in addition to leap-frog development. Fujita [1983] summarizes all these "descriptive" models of residential growth with perfect foresight and further examines a generalized version of the Fujita–Wheaton model with many types of buildings and activities to demonstrate that competition under perfect foresight may lead to all sorts of sprawl-fashioned development such as leap-frog, mixed and scattered development patterns.

Interestingly, these sprawl patterns can be Pareto optimal in an intertemporal sense, as shown in Ohls and Pines [1975], Pines [1976], and Fujita [1976a, 1976b], which assume the durability and adjustment costs of housing capital and investigate the optimal process of residential growth and land development. Specifically, Fujita considers a monocentric city with many types of houses and households located in many concentric rings, where each type of housing can be characterized by its structure and lot size. Then, his dynamic optimization problem is to maximize the present value of the net rent revenue from residential development in the city as a whole, given a utility stream for each type of household. Any solution to this optimization problem with an arbitrarily given utility stream is shown to be a competitive market solution, where each developer has perfect foresight and maximizes the present value of the net revenue per unit of land for housing of each type in each ring, and each household maximizes its utility subject to the budget constraint with an appropriately chosen income subsidy or tax. Conversely, for any given set of income subsidy or tax for each household type, there exists a certain utility stream for each household type such that the optimization problem has a solution which coincides with the competitive solution for the given values of income subsidy or tax. In this sense, the set of optimal solutions is equivalent to the set of competitive solutions. It is further shown that urban sprawl such as leap-frog, mixed, and scattered development patterns can be a solution to the optimization problem for some utility stream.

Similar optimality results are obtained in Ripper and Varaiya [1974] and Pines and Werczberger [1982] which employ a linear programming method to analyze dynamic urban land use, where Fujita's optimum control approach is adopted in Hochman and Pines [1980, 1982] to compare optimal and competitive development patterns under the assumption of flexible dwelling unit size. By virtue of this assumption, land rents and densities are always declining with greater commuting distance in the Hochman–Pines model. This is in contrast to Fujita's result [1982, 1983], where there is a possibility of positive rent and density gradients in the case of fixed dwelling size. Akita and Fujita [1982], Fujita [1983], and Pines and Werczberger [1982] obtain both optimal and competitive solutions in the presence of urban renewal and upgrading. Their analyses indicate a wide variety of equilibrium development patterns, including sprawl patterns, which are also socially optimal.

6. SUGGESTIONS FOR FUTURE RESEARCH

There seem to be many ways in which the existing dynamic urban models can be modified and improved. First of all, it is clear that most of the dynamic urban production models are rather primitive in that those models do not take account of the durability of structure or the role of expectations, as in some of the urban residential models. Given the recent developments in the residential models surveyed above, it should not be too difficult to construct a dynamic production model with explicit attention paid to durability and expectations in a spatial setting, and such a model would be quite useful in gaining insight into the dynamic process of industrial growth and adjustment in a large metropolitan area.

Related to the above point is the necessity to integrate the production and employment aspects into the residential model of urban growth more fully. As already mentioned, there exist very few urban models which incorporate both production and residential activities in space in a satisfactory fashion. This gap between the production models and the residential models must be filled in order to deal with many important issues involving both industry and residents, e.g., how to allocate scare urban land between industrial use and residential development in a growing city from a long-term viewpoint. Needless to say, one could not tell a whole story about urban growth and development without analyzing the dynamic interaction between industrial and residential activities in an integrated model of urban production and housing.

In this connection, the monocentric city assumption seems very restrictive and unrealistic and hence should be replaced with the assumption of a multicentric city, where the size and the number of business centres are endogenously determined. Only within the multicentric city framework with production/employment centers growing in size and number through time, the dynamic interaction among industrial production, employment location, housing consumption, and travel choice could be effectively analyzed, and many policy implications relevant to real urban problems might be likely to follow from such analysis. It will be worthwhile to extend the existing urban growth models in this direction by allowing a number of subcenters in the previously monocentric city, as seen in Fujita and Ogawa [1982].

There is no need to stress the fact that a city cannot live by itself. Especially in the dynamic context, the analysis of a single city, which is assumed either closed or open, is not quite satisfactory and should be regarded as a first step toward a more general treatment of a city which interacts and grows with the rest of the whole system. At least some of the existing models on a system of cities, regional growth and development, and rural-urban migration try to capture the interrelation among a group of cities as well as between a city and its surrounding region. In such a framework, one can gain more insight into the underlying reasons for urban growth such as inter-city specialization and factor movements into and out of a city. It will, therefore, be useful to reexamine the existing models in these fields and integrate some of their relevant aspects into the dynamic theory of urban growth and adjustment.

It is easy to say more about possible extensions and modifications of the existing models, but is very difficult to do it in a satisfactory way, because many of the existing urban dynamic models are already quite complicated in analysis. Analytical difficulty and intractability are preventing many more meaningful variables from being introduced into these models. Especially, it would be desirable to incorporate more policy variables in the existing models in order to derive policy implications of the theoretical analyses which are reviewed above. One possible way of doing it is to employ a numerical simulation method as has been used by some authors in this field. Urban simulation models can be more fully utilized in order to enrich the field of urban growth and dynamics (See Anas [1986]).

As already mentioned in the Introduction, this survey has focused on dynamic models which present some analytical framework, and not on less analytical but often broader approaches to the subject such as Jacobs [1970]. As a possible future development, however, one cannot ignore the importance of addressing fundamental questions about the historical developments of urban regions. We must find a reasonable way to deal with some of the basic factors for urban growth, decay, and possibly death from a "super" long-run viewpoint. It will probably be necessary to turn to some unorthodox concepts and techniques, e.g., catastrophe theory, for formalizing the ideas and intuition which have been gained from those broader approaches in the existing literature.

Finally, the field of urban growth and dynamics has been expanding very rapidly in the last few years, and more work is being done while this survey article is in press. The present survey, therefore, is bound to be obsolete at least some extent by the time it is published. In order to supplement the contents of this survey with updated materials, the reader is urged to read the most recent issues of major journals in urban economics and regional science. Hopefully, some articles in those issues will have already taken account of the points made in this concluding section.

References

Akita, T. and M. Fujita [1982], "Spatial Development Process with Renewal in a Growing City," *Environment and Planning A,* **14,** 205–223.

Alonso, W. [1964], *Location and Land Use,* Cambridge, Mass., Harvard University Press.

Anas, A. [1976], "Short-run Dynamics in the Spatial Housing Market," in G. J. Papageorgiou, ed., *Mathematical Land Use Theory,* Lexington, Mass., D. C. Heath, 261–275.

Anas, A. [1978], "Dynamics of Urban Residential Growth," *Journal of Urban Edonomics,* **5,** 66–87.

Anas, A. [1986], "Economic Urban and Regional Simulation," in J. Lesourne and H. Sonnenschein, eds., *Fundamentals of Pure and Applied Economics* and *Encyclopedia of Economics,* Paris, Harwood Academic Publishers.

Anderson, R. J. [1970], "A Note on Economic Base Studies and Regional Econometric Forecasting Models," *Journal of Regional Science,* **10,** 325–333.

Arnott, R. J. [1980], "A Simple Urban Growth Model with Durable Housing," *Regional Science and Urban Economics,* **10,** 53–76.

Beckmann, M. J. [1972], "Von Thunen Revisited: A Neoclassical Land Use Model," *Swedish Journal of Economics,* **74,** 1–7.

Bell, G. H. [1967], "An Econometric Forecasting Model for a Region," *Journal of Regional Science,* **7,** 109–127.

Borts, G. H. [1971], "Growth and Capital Movements Among United States Regions in the Postwar Period," in J. F. Kain and J. R. Meyer, eds., *Essays in Regional Economics,* Cambridge, Mass., Harvard University Press, 189–217.

Borts, G. H. and J. L. Stein [1964], *Economic Growth in a Free Market,* New York, Columbia University Press.

Brueckner, J. K. [1980a], "A Vintage Model of Urban Growth," *Journal of Urban Economics,* **8,** 389–402.

Brueckner, J. K. [1981], "A Dynamic Model of Housing Production," *Journal of Urban Economics,* **10,** 1–14.

Brueckner, J. K. and B. v. Rabenau [1981], "Dynamics of Land Use for a Closed City," *Regional Science and Urban Economics,* **11,** 1–17.

Carlberg, M. [1981], "An Economic Growth Model of the Productive City," in P.

Nijkamp and P. Rietveld, eds., *Cities in Transition: Problems and Policies.* Alphen ann den Rijn, The Netherlands, Sijthoff & Noordhoff, 271–293.

Casetti, E. [1980], "Equilibrium Population Partitions Between Urban and Agricultural Occupations," *Geographical Analysis,* **12,** 47–54.

Conroy, M. E. [1975], *The Challenge of Urban Economic Development,* Lexington, Mass., D. C. Heath.

Czamanski, S. [1964], "A Model of Urban Growth," *Papers of the Regional Science Association,* **13,** 177–200.

Czamanski, S. [1965], "A Method of Forecasting Metropolitan Growth by Means of Distributed Lags Analysis," *Journal of Regional Science,* **6,** 35–49.

Day, R. H. and E. H. Tinney [1969], "A Dynamic von Thunen Model," *Geographical Analysis,* **1,** 137–151.

Day, R. H. and P. E. Kennedy [1970], "On a Dynamic Location Model of Production," *Journal of Regional Science,* **10,** 191–197.

Day, R. H., P. E. Kennedy, and E. H. Tinney [1978], "A Cobweb Version of the von Thunen Model," in R. H. Day and A. Cigno, eds., *Modelling Economic Change: The Recursive Programming Approach,* Amsterdam, North-Holland, 217–231.

Dendrinos, D. S. [1982], "On the Dynamic Stability of Interurban/Regional Labor and Capital Movements," *Journal of Regional Science,* **22,** 529–540.

Dixon, R. and A. P. Thirlwall [1975], "A Model of Regional Growth-Rate Differences on Kaldorian Lines," *Oxford Economic Papers,* **27,** 201–214.

Engle, R. F., F. M. Fisher, J. R. Harris, and J. Rothenberg [1972], "An Econometric Simulation Model of Intra-Metropolitan Housing Location: Housing, Business, Transportation and Local Government," *American Economic Review,* **62,** 87–97.

Engle, R. F. [1974], "Issues in the Specification of an Econometric Model of Metropolitan Growth," *Journal of Urban Economics,* **1,** 250–267.

Evans, A. W. [1975], "Rent and Housing in the Theory of Urban Growth," *Journal of Regional Science,* **15,** 113–125.

Friedmann, J. and W. Alonso [1964], *Regional Development and Planning: A Reader,* Cambridge, Mass., MIT Press.

Fujita, M. [1976a], "Spatial Patterns of Urban Growth: Optimum and Market," *Journal of Urban Economics,* **3,** 209–241.

Fujita, M. [1976b], "Toward a Dynamic Theory of Urban Land Use," *Papers of the Regional Science Association,* **37,** 133–165.

Fujita, M. [1982], "Spatial Patterns of Residential Development," *Journal of Urban Economics,* **12,** 22–52.

Fujita, M. [1983], "Urban Spatial Dynamics: A Survey," *Sistemi Urban,* **5**.

Fujita, M. [1986], "Urban Land Use Theory," in J. Lesourne and H. Sonnenschein, eds. *Fundamentals of Pure and Applied Economics* and *Encyclopedia of Economics,* Paris, Harwood Academic Publishers.

Fujita, M. and H. Ogawa [1982], "Multiple Equilibria and Structural Transition of Non-monocentric Urban Configurations," *Regional Science and Urban Economics,* **12,** 161–196.

Glickman, N. J. [1971], "An Econometric Forecasting Model for the Philadelphia Region," *Journal of Regional Science,* **11,** 15–32.

Greenwood, M. J. [1973], "Urban Economic Growth and Migration: Their Interaction," *Environment and Planning,* **5,** 91–112.

Hall, O. P. and J. A. Licari [1974], "Building Small Region Econometric Models: Extension of Glickman's Structure to Los Angeles," *Journal of Regional Science,* **14,** 337–353.

Harrison, D. and J. F. Kain [1974], "Cumulative Urban Growth and Urban Density Functions," *Journal of Urban Economics,* **1,** 61–98.

Hartwick, J., U. Schweizer, and P. Varaiya [1976a], "Comparative Statics of a Residential Economy with Several Classes," in G. J. Papageorgiou, ed., *Mathematical Land Use Theory,* Lexington, Mass., D. C. Heath, 55–78.

Hartwick, J., U. Schweizer, and P. Varaiya [1976b], "Comparative Statics of a Residential Economy with Several Classes," *Journal of Economic Theory,* **13,** 396–413.

Harvey, A. S. [1974], "A Dualistic Model of Urban Growth," *The Annals of Regional Science,* **8,** 58–69.

Hochman, O. and D. Pines [1980], "Costs of Adjustment and Demolition Costs in Residential Construction and Their Effects of Urban Growth," *Journal of Urban Economics,* **7,** 2–19.

Hochman, O. and D. Pines [1982], "Costs of Adjustment and the Spatial Pattern of a Growing Open City," *Econometrica,* **50,** 1371–1389.

Isard, W. and Y. Kanemoto [1976], "Stages in Space-Time Development," *Papers of the Regional Science Association,* **37,** 99–131.

Jacobs, J. [1970], *The Economy of Cities,* New York, Random House.

Kaldor, N. [1970], "The Case for Regional Policies," *Scottish Journal of Political Econopmy,* **17,** 337–348.

Kanemoto, Y. [1980a], "Externality, Migration, and Urban Crises," *Journal of Urban Economics,* **8,** 150–164.

Kanemoto, Y. [1980b], *Theories of Urban Externalities,* Amsterdam, North-Holland.

Kanemoto, Y. [1986], "Externalities in Space," in J. Lesourne and H. Sonnenschein, eds. *Fundamentals of Pure and Applied Economics* and *Encyclopedia of Economics,* Paris, Harwood Academic Publishers.

Klein, L. R. [1969], "The Specification of Regional Econometric Models," *Papers of the Regional Science Association,* **23,** 105–115.

Lewis, W. C. and J. R. Prescott [1972], "Urban-Regional Development and Growth Centers: An Econometric Study," *Journal of Regional Science,* **12,** 57–70.

Mazek, W. F. and J. Chang [1972], "The Chicken and Egg Fowl-up in Migration: Comment," *Southern Economic Journal,* **39,** 133–139.

Mills, D. E. [1981], "Growth, Speculation and Sprawl in a Monocentric City," *Journal of Urban Economics,* **10,** 201–226.

Mills, E. S. [1967], "An Aggregative Model of Resource Allocation in a Metropolitan Area," *American Economic Review,* **57,** 197–210.

Miron, J. R. [1979], "Migration and Urban Economic Growth," *Regional Science and Urban Economics,* **9,** 159–183.

Miyao, T. [1975], "Dynamics and Comparative Statics in the Theory of Residential Location," *Journal of Economic Theory,* **11,** 133–146.

Miyao, T. [1977a], "Some Dynamic and Comparative Static Properties of a Spatial Model of Production," *Review of Economic Studies,* **44,** 321–327.

Miyao, T. [1977b], "A Long-run Analysis of Urban Growth over Space," *Canadian Journal of Economics,* **10,** 678–686.

Miyao, T. [1977c], "The Golden Rule of Urban Transportation Investment," *Journal of Urban Economics,* **4,** 448–458.

Miyao, T. [1978], "Dynamic Instability of a Mixed City in the Presence of Neighborhood Externalities," *American Economic Review,* **68,** 454–463.

Miyao, T. [1979], "Dynamic Stability of an Open City with Many Household Classes," *Journal of Urban Economics,* **8,** 222–235.

Miyao, T. [1980], "Dynamics of Metropolitan Growth and Unemployment," *Journal of Urban Economics,* **8,** 222–235.

Miyao, T. [1981], *Dynamic Analysis of the Urban Economy,* New York, Academic Press.

Miyao, T. [1983], "Rural and Urban Population Changes and the Stages of Economic Development: A Unified Approach," *Environment and Planning A,* **15,** 1161–1174.

Miyao, T., P. Shapiro, and D. Knapp [1980], "On the Existence, Uniqueness, and Stability of Spatial Equilibrium in an Open City with Externalities," *Journal of Urban Economics,* **8,** 139–149.

Moody, H. T. and F. W. Puffer [1969], "A Gross Regional Product Approach to Regional Model-Building," *Western Economic Journal,* **7,** 391–402.

Moody, H. T. and F. W. Puffer [1970], "The Empirical Verification of the Urban Base Multiplier: Traditional and Adjustment Process Models," *Land Economics,* **46,** 91–98.

Muth, R. F. [1968], "Differential Growth Among Large U.S. Cities," in J. P. Quirk and A. M. Zarley, eds., *Papers in Quantitative Economics,* Lawrence, University Press of Kansas.

Muth, R. F. [1969], *Cities and Housing,* Chicago, University of Chicago Press.

Muth, R. F. [1971], "Migration: Chicken or Egg?" *Southern Economic Journal,* **37,** 295–306.

Muth, R. F. [1972], "The Chicken or Egg Fowl-up in Migration: Reply," *Southern Economic Journal,* **39,** 139–142.

Muth, R. F. [1973], "A Vintage Model of the Housing Stock," *Papers of the Regional Science Association,* **30,** 141–156.

Myrdal, G. [1957], *Economic Theory and Under-Developed Regions,* London, Gerald Ducknorth.

Niedercorn, J. H. [1963], "An Econometric Model of Metropolitan Employment and Population Growth," EM-3758-RC, Santa Monica, RAND Corporation.

Niedercorn, J. H. and J. F. Kain [1963], "An Econometric Model of Metropolitan Development," *Papers and Proceedings of the Regional Science Association,* **11,** 123–143.

Ohls, J. C. and D. Pines [1975], "Continuous Urban Development and Economic Efficiency," *Land Economics,* **51,** 224–234.

Okabe, A. and Y. Kume [1983], "A Dynamic von Thunen Model with a Demand Function," *Journal of Urban Economics,* **14,** 355–369.

Okun, B. [1968], "Interstate Population Migration and State Income Inequality: A Simultaneous Equation Approach," *Economic Development and Cultural Change,* **16,** 297–313.

Paelinck, J. [1970], "Dynamic Urban Growth Models," *Papers of the Regional Science Association,* **24,** 25–37.

Papageorgiou, G. J. [1980], "On Sudden Urban Growth," *Environment and Planning A,* **12,** 1035–1050.

Pfouts, R. W. [1960], *The Techniques of Urban Economic Analysis,* West Trenton, New Jersey, Chandler-Davis.

Pines, D. [1976], "Dynamic Aspects of Land Use Patterns in a Growing City," in G. J. Papageorgiou ed., *Mathematical Land Use Theory,* Lexington, Mass., D. C. Heath, 229–243.

Pines, D. and E. Werczberger [1982], "A Linear Programming Model of the Urban Housing and Land Markets: Static and Dynamic Aspects," *Regional Science and Urban Economics,* **12,** 211–233.

Rabenau, B. v. [1976], "Optimal Growth of a Factory Town," *Journal of Urban Economics,* **3,** 97–112.

Rabenau, B. v. [1979], "Urban Growth with Agglomeration Economies and Diseconomies," *Geographia Polonica,* **42,** 77–90.
Rabenau, B. v. and D. A. Hanson [1979], "The Provision of Public Goods in a Growing Urban Economy," *Regional Science and Urban Economics,* **9,** 1–20.
Richardson, H. W. [1971], *Urban Economics,* Harmondsworth, England, Penguin.
Richardson, H. W. [1973], *Regional Growth Theory,* New York, John Wiley.
Richardson, H. W. [1978], "The State of Regional Economics: A Survey Article," *International Regional Science Review,* **3,** 1–48.
Ripper, M. and P. Varaiya [1974], "An Optimizing Model of Urban Development," *Environment and Planning A,* **6,** 149–168.
Romans, J. T. [1965], *Capital Exports and Growth Among U.S. Regions,* Middletown, Conn., Wesleyan University Press.
Schelling, T. C. [1969], "Models of Segregation," *American Economic Review,* **59,** 488–493.
Schelling, T. C. [1971], "Dynamic Models of Segregation," *Journal of Mathematical Sociology,* **1,** 143–186.
Siebert, H. [1969], *Regional Economic Growth: Theory and Policy,* Scranton, Penn., International Textbook.
Smith, D. M. [1974], "Regional Growth: Interstate and Intersectoral Factor Reallocation," *Review of Economics and Statistics,* **61,** 353–359.
Smith, D. M. [1975], "Neoclassical Growth Models and Regional Growth in the U.S.," *Journal of Regional Science,* **15,** 165–181.
Solow, R. M. [1973], "On Equilibrium Models of Urban Location," in M. Parkin, ed., *Essays in Modern Economics,* London, Longman Group, 2–16.
Thompson, W. R. [1965], *A Preface to Urban Economics,* Baltimore, Johns Hopkins Press.
Vousden, N. [1980], "An Open-City Model with Nonmalleable Housing," *Journal of Urban Economics,* **7,** 248–277.
Wheaton, W. C. [1974], "A Comparative Static Analysis of Urban Spatial Structure," *Journal of Urban Economics,* **9,** 223–237.
Wheaton, W. C. [1982a], "Urban Spatial Development with Durable but Replaceable Capital," *Journal of Urban Economics,* **12,** 53–67.
Wheaton, W. C. [1982b], "Urban Residential Growth under Perfect Foresight," *Journal of Urban Economics,* **12,** 1–21.
Wheaton, W. C. [1983], "Theories of Urban Growth and Metropolitan Spatial Development," in J. V. Henderson, ed., *Research in Urban Economics,* Vol. 3, Greenwich. Conn., JAI Press. 3–36.

Externalities in Space

YOSHITSUGU KANEMOTO[1]
University of Tsukuba

1. INTRODUCTION

Cities are usually defined as densely populated geographic areas and a concentration of many people in a small area causes many types of externalities such as traffic congestion, racial discrimination, pollution, noises, and neighborhood amenities. This article surveys recent developments in the economic analysis of urban externalities. Since space plays a key role in urban living, our attention is focused on the spatial aspect of urban externalities.

"Externalities" arise when one economic agent does not compensate others for his actions which may directly affect their consumption or production possibilities. Smokers who do not, for example, pay for increasing others' risks of cancer, or for the discomfort they may cause, produce externalities. Urban life is filled with examples of externalities: manufacturing producers may cause air and water pollution which negatively affects city residents and other producers; some individuals may have a racial prejudice against certain ethnic groups; a household may benefit from beautiful gardens of its neighbours; firms often prefer to locate in larger cities because of proximity to other firms; and an additional traveller in a congested road imposes external costs on other

[1] A previous version of this article has been presented at a Workshop on Urban and Regional Economics at Queen's University, a Workshop on Public Economics at the National Institute of Public Finance, and a Workshop on Regional Science at the University of Tsukuba. I am grateful for the participants of the workshops for useful comments. A travel grant from Yoshida International Education Foundation which enabled me to attend the first Workshop is gratefully acknowledged. Special thanks are due to Richard Arnott for many valuable comments. I also wish to thank Sandra Boyle for editorial assistance.

travellers by slowing them down. According to the *Fundamental Theorem of Welfare Economics,* a competitive equilibrium is efficient in the Pareto optimal sense if all goods are private goods and no externalities exist. This result, however, breaks down if there are externalities. An individual decision maker who generates externalities does not take into account external costs (or benefits) imposed on others. His decision must therefore be corrected to account for external effects. If, for example, the externality is harmful, the generating agent should be induced to diminish the externality compared with what private self-intesest would dictate. Externalities thus present a case of potential market failure where government intervention may be called for to guide a decentralized market system toward a point where resource allocation is efficient.

It is, however, too early to jump to the conclusion that government actions are always justified when there are externalities. For example, individuals who suffer from water pollution have an incentive to get together and bribe firms to reduce pollution. The reason why this may not happen is that the transactions costs to set up a market for pollution may be too high. If the government has to incur the same transactions costs as private individuals, then government intervention cannot improve resource allocation. Government intervention is justified, therefore, only if the coercive power of the government reduces the transactions costs.

Even if government intervention is justifiable, the government has to choose an appropriate policy among alternative policy measures. For example, introducing a Pigouvian tax/subsidy system is one way of modifying individual actions to achieve an efficient allocation. A tax placed on pollution will tend to reduce the amount of externality. If a corrective tax is set equal to the marginal externality costs suffered by others, an efficient allocation is attained. One problem with the Pigouvian tax/subsidy, however, is that it usually requires high administrative costs. In some cases, direct regulation of private activities such as a ceiling on pollution emissions and a control of land use may be less costly. Moreover, the government might also have to resort to cruder measures. For example, a Pigouvian tax/subsidy system for traffic congestion requires congestion tolls whose levels are different for different roads depending on the severity of congestion. Implementation of such a system is obviously very costly and the only practical policy tool may be a uniform gasoline tax whose rate is the same in all roads. In this situation, we see that while the uniform tax is an imperfect tool, it may still be better than no tax at all.

If the government has only imperfect tools (or none at all) to deal with externalities, the 'first-best' Pareto optimal allocation will not be achieved and we will subsequently face a complicated 'second-best' problem. For example, if no congestion tolls are imposed on traffic congestion, or if only a uniform gasoline tax is levied, then the appropriate benefit-cost criterion for building roads is no longer the same as one which is valid in the first-best world. This problem is discussed in Section 4 on externalities associated with transportation.

In this article, urban externalities are classified according to the types of agents who cause and receive the externalities: externalities from producers to households; externalities among households; externalities among producers; and externalities associated with urban transportation. The first four sections review contributions on these four types of externalities separately.

Section 2 deals mainly with air pollution externalities. In a spatial model of pollution, land use control, in addition to the Pigouvian tax, might be necessary to achieve an efficient allocation.

In Section 3, externalities associated with racial prejudice and housing upkeep are considered. Major issues in the spatial analyses of racial prejudice are: (1) what sort of a spatial pattern (an integrated, segregated or some other pattern) is necessary for a stable equilibrium, and (2) is there a possibility of dynamic instability when a small increase in the population of one ethnic group drives away the other ethnic group, causing a sudden change in the racial composition? Housing upkeep externalities refer to external benefits from good housing maintenance which are enjoyed by neighborhood residents.

External economies among producers, which are reviewed in Section 4, are considered as one of the major reasons why cities exist. We review two types of models: one which assumes that firms in the same city receive the same amount of external economies regardless of where in the CBD they are located and another which assumes that firms receive more externalities by locating closer to other firms even inside the CBD.

In Section 5, two types of externalities associated with urban transportation are considered: traffic congestion which represents externalities among travellers, and externalities which urban transportation imposes on city residents.

The first four sections are mostly theoretical, although related empirical works are mentioned when necessary. Empirical work related to the estimation of benefits and costs of externalities is reviewed in Section 6.

2. EXTERNALITIES BETWEEN PRODUCERS AND HOUSEHOLDS

Industrial production often causes external diseconomies which negatively affect city residents. For example, households in a residential area which is located close to a number of chemical plants typically suffer from air pollution. Externalities of this type have been analyzed by Stull [100], Henderson [36, 37], Helpman and Pines [34], Hochman and Ofek [41], and Miyao, Shapiro, and Knapp [62]. Major economic issues examined in these works include:

- the effects of externalities on the spatial structure of a city;
- the comparison between optimal and market allocations;
- the appropriate policies which are necessary to control externalities, e.g., Pigouvian taxes, emission standards, and land use regulation; and
- the existence, uniqueness, and stability of competitive equilibrium with externalities.

Consider a monocentric city on a featureless plain, where producers are located in a central business district (CBD) which is surrounded by a residential zone. Let x denote distance from the city center. The industrial zone extends from radius 0 to radius $\underline{x}$ and the residential zone from $\underline{x}$ to $\bar{x}$, where $0 \leqq \underline{x} \leqq \bar{x}$. It turns out that there may be a green belt between residential and industrial zones. In such a case, $\underline{x}$ denotes the edge of the industrial zone and a green belt is between $\underline{x}$ and x^*, where $\underline{x} \leqq x^* \leqq \bar{x}$.

All producers have the same production function, $F(N, H, K, e)$, where N, H, and K are respectively the amounts of labor, land, and capital inputs, and e is the quantity of pollution emitted by the producer. Pollution abatement activities are embedded in the production function and pollution is treated as a factor of production. An increase in pollution increases production because less inputs are required for anti-pollution activity. The production function is assumed to be homogeneous of degree one. Since firm size is indeterminate under this assumption, firms are identified by distance from the city center. This implies that the amount of land input used by a firm at x is the total available land at x, denoted by $\bar{H}(x)$.

All city residents have the same utility function, $U(z, h, a)$, where z and h are, respectively, the amounts of the composite consumer good and residential land, and a is the level of pollution. The pollution level depends on the amounts of pollutants emitted by the industrial sector. It also depends on distance from producers because pollutants diffuse and dissipate as they move farther from the industrial zone. In general, the pollution level at x, $a(x)$, depends on the distribution of pollution emission in the industrial zone, $e(x')$, $0 \leqq x' \leqq \underline{x}$, and the location of residence, x. It can therefore be written that $a(x) = A(\langle e(x')\rangle, x)$, where $\langle e(x')\rangle$ denotes the entire profile of $e(x')$ in the industrial sector.

The specification of the pollution function (or, more precisely, the functional), $A(\ )$, has important consequences on the spatial structure of the city. Stull [100] assumed that the pollution level depends only on distance from the border of the industrial zone, i.e., $a(x) = A(x - \underline{x})$ with $A'(x - \underline{x}) < 0$. This formulation ignores the effect of the quantity of pollutants. Henderson [36, 37] and Helpman and Pines [34] extended the formulation to include the quantity effect. Henderson's specification is most general. The pollution level at the industrial-residential boundary is first obtained. The emissions of a firm at radius x', $e(x')$, dissipate before reaching the boundary and their contribution to pollution there is $g(e(x'), x', \underline{x})$. An increase in emissions of course increases pollution, i.e., $\partial g/\partial e > 0$, and a given level of emissions contributes more to pollution if they come from a firm closer to the boundary, i.e., $\partial g/\partial x' > 0$. Also, $\partial g/\partial \underline{x} < 0$, or as the industrial zone expands, the emissions of a firm at a given location x' are more dispersed before they reach the boundary. The total pollutants at the boundary are the sum of contributions by all firms in the CBD,

$$E(\underset{\sim}{x}) = \int_0^{\underset{\sim}{x}} g(e(x'), x', \underset{\sim}{x})\, dx'. \tag{2.1}$$

These pollutants are evenly distributed over all points on the boundary. The pollution level at radius x in the residential zone is then a function of the pollution level at the boundary and distance from the boundary,

$$a(x) = A[E(\underset{\sim}{x}), x, \underset{\sim}{x}], \tag{2.2}$$

where $\partial A/\partial E > 0$, $\partial A/\partial x < 0$, and $\partial A/\partial \underset{\sim}{x} > 0$.

Henderson's formulation treats the industrial and residential zones differently because dissipation in the industrial zone is captured by function $g(\ )$ and that in the residential zone by function $A(\ )$. If we treat the two zones symmetrically, the contribution of emissions at x' to pollution at x can be written $g(e(x'), x', x)$ and the total pollutants at x are

$$a(x) = \int_0^{\underset{\sim}{x}} g(e(x'), x', x)\, dx'. \tag{2.3}$$

This formulation is adopted by Yellin [109] and Kanemoto [46] in models of racial prejudice.

An individual who lives at x and works for a firm at x' has the budget constraint,

$$y(x') = z(x) + R(x)h(x) + t(x - x'), \tag{2.4}$$

where $y(x')$, $R(x)$, and $t(x - x')$ are respectively income, land rent, and commuting costs. For simplicity, commuting costs are assumed to be linear with respect to commuting distance. The income, $y(x')$, includes the wage, $w(x')$, and other fixed income, s, i.e., $y(x') = w(x') + s$. It is assumed that all residents have the same ability and the same utility function, and, as a consequence, the utility levels are equal regardless of where they live and where they work. This implies that firms farther from the residential zone must exactly compensate the commuting cost differentials by higher wages, i.e., $y(x') = y + t(\underset{\sim}{x} - x')$, where $y = y(\underset{\sim}{x})$ is the income of an individual who works at $\underset{\sim}{x}$. The wage, $w(x')$, also satisfies $w(x') = w + t(\underset{\sim}{x} - x')$, where $w = w(\underset{\sim}{x})$.

A household at x maximizes its utility, $U(z, h, a(x))$, subject to the budget constraint, $y = z + R(x)h + t(x - \underset{\sim}{x})$, where the choice variables are the amounts of the consumer good, z, and land, h. The optimal choice of z and h then depends on income net of commuting costs, $y - t(x - \underline{x})$, land rent, $R(x)$, and the pollution level, $a(x)$, and can be written $z(x) = z^*(y - t(x - \underline{x}), R(x), a(x))$ and $h(x) = h^*(y - t(x - \underline{x}), R(x), a(x))$. Substituting these equations into the utility function yields the indirect utility function, $v(y - t(x - \underline{x}), R(x), a(x)) = U[z^*(y - t(x - \underline{x}), R(x), a(x)), h^*(y - t(x - \underline{x}), R(x), a(x)), a(x)]$. The bid rent function which represents the maximum land rent that a household can pay while attaining a certain utility level, u, is then $R(y - t(x - \underline{x}), a(x), u)$, where the bid rent function satisfies the identity, $v[y - t(x - \underline{x}), R(y - t(x - \underline{x}), a(x), u), a(x)] \equiv u$. If the utility level is the same as that obtained in equilibrium, then the bid rent function yields the equilibrium rent profile. In a model with pollution, the bid rent depends on the pollution level as well as net income and the utility level. Obviously, the bid rent is lower if the pollution level is higher, or $\delta R/\delta a < 0$ if $\delta U/\delta a < 0$.

A firm at x' ships its product to the city center. The price at the center is fixed at p and the net price at x' after subtracting transport costs is denoted by $p(x')$. Then the profit of the firm is $p(x')F(N, \bar{H}(x'), K, e) - w(x')N - R(x')\bar{H}(x') - r_K K - \tau(x')e$, where r_K is the rental rate of capital input which is assumed to be constant throughout the city, $\tau(x')$ is the Pigouvian tax rate on pollution emissions at x', and $\bar{H}(x')$ is the available land at x'. The profit maximizing input levels are then $N(x') = N^*(p(x'), w(x'), r_K, \tau(x'), \bar{H}(x'))$, $K(x') = K^*(p(x'), w(x'), r_K, \tau(x'), \bar{H}(x'))$, and $e(x') = e^*(p(x'), w(x'), r_K, \tau(x'), \bar{H}(x'))$. Notice that the level of land rent does not affect the optimal amounts of inputs because land input is fixed. In long-run equilibrium, land rent is determined so that profit is zero:

$$\begin{aligned} R(x') &= \frac{1}{\bar{H}(x')}[p(x')F - w(x')N - r_K K - \tau(x')e] \\ &= R[p(x'), w(x'), r_K, \tau(x'), \bar{H}(x')]. \end{aligned}$$

Next, the total supply of labor in the city must equal the total demand,

$$\int_0^{\underline{x}} N(x')\,dx' = \int_{\underline{x}}^{\bar{x}} N(x)\,dx, \qquad (2.5)$$

where $N(x)$ denotes the number of workers at x in the industrial zone and the number of residents in the residential zone. The number of residents must satisfy $\bar{H}(x) = N(x)h(x)$, where $\bar{H}(x)$ is the amount of land available for residence at x. The edge of the residential zone, $\bar{x}$, is determined in such a way that the residential rent there equals the fixed rural rent, $R(\bar{x}) = R_a$.

In order to close the model we need to specify land ownership and openness of the city. For example, a city may be small and open with absentee ownership of land or closed with land owned by the city government. However, we first examine a number of properties which do not depend on these conditions.

The optimal solution requires Pigouvian taxes on pollution emissions. The tax rate equals the externality costs that an additional unit of emissions imposes on city residents. The costs depend on the specification of the pollution function, $A(\ )$.

In Stull's formulation, $a(x) = A(x - \underline{x})$, the pollution level does not depend on the quantity of emissions and the tax rate is zero.

In Henderson's formulation, $a(x) = A[\int_0^{\underline{x}} g(e(x'), x', \underline{x})\, dx', x, \underline{x}]$, and a marginal increase in emissions at x' raises the pollution level at x by $(\partial A(E, x, \underline{x})/\partial E)(\partial g/\partial e(x'))$. The social benefit of a unit increase in pollution at x, which is less than zero, is the marginal rate of substitution between pollution and the consumer good multiplied by the number of residents at x, $[(\partial U/\partial a)/(\partial U/\partial z)]N(x)$. The total social cost of a unit increase in emissions at x' is the sum of social costs at all locations in the residential zone. As a consequence, the pollution tax can be written as:

$$\tau(x') = -\int_{\underline{x}}^{\bar{x}} \frac{\partial U/\partial a}{\partial U/\partial z} \frac{\partial A}{\partial E} N(x) \frac{\partial g}{\partial e(x')}\, dx. \tag{2.6}$$

This result shows that, in general, the tax rate is location dependent. The administration of the Pigouvian tax system therefore requires detailed information on the spatial structure of pollution diffusion. The Pigouvian tax rate in Henderson's model is, however, uniform and does not depend on the location of the producer. The difference between these results is due to the fact that the tax in Henderson's model is not levied on the emission level at the production site but on the contribution of an individual producer's emissions to the pollution level at the industrial-residential boundary, $g(e(x'), x', \bar{x})$. Since (2.6) can be decomposed into

$$\tau(x') = \tau[\partial g/\partial e(x')], \tag{2.7}$$

where

$$\tau = -\int_{\underline{x}}^{\bar{x}} \frac{\partial U/\partial a}{\partial U/\partial z} \frac{\partial A}{\partial E} N(x)\, dx, \tag{2.8}$$

the optimal solution can be implemented by a uniform tax on the contribution to pollution at the boundary. It is, however, more difficult to observe the contribution than the emissions at the production site, although even the latter is not easy to observe.

Finally, in the symmetric formulation (2.3), the total marginal cost of an increase in emissions at x', which equals the Pigouvian tax rate, is

$$\tau(x') = -\int_{\underline{x}}^{\bar{x}} \frac{\partial U/\partial a}{\partial U/\partial z} N(x) \frac{\partial g(e(x'), x', x)}{\partial e(x')}\, dx. \tag{2.9}$$

Here the tax rate varies depending on the location of the firm. Unlike in Henderson's formulation, a uniform tax on the contribution to pollution at the boundary does not in general yield the optimal solution, since the right hand side of (2.9) does not have a decomposition like (2.7).

Next, for the CBD boundary to be optimal, the social benefit of a marginal increase in $\underline{x}$ must equal the social cost (i.e., the benefit derived from expanding the industrial zone is completely offset by the cost of contracting the residential zone). The social benefit of a unit increase in $\underline{x}$ is the value of output minus the costs of capital and labor inputs minus the social cost of increased pollution, i.e.,

$$B = p(\underline{x})F(N(\underline{x}^-), H(\underline{x}), K(\underline{x}), e(\underline{x})) - r_K k(\underline{x}) - wN(\underline{x}^-) - D,$$

where D denotes the social cost of increased pollution which depends on the specification of the pollution function. Since $N(x)$ means the number of workers employed at x inside $\underline{x}$ and the number of residents outside $\underline{x}$, it in general has a jump at $\underline{x}$. $N(\underline{x}^-)$ denotes the left side limit, or the number of workers at $\underline{x}$, and $N(\underline{x}^+)$ the right side limit, or the number of residents at $\underline{x}$. By the linear homogeneity of the production function, the benefit can be rewritten as $B = R(\underline{x}^-)\bar{H}(\underline{x}) + \tau(\underline{x})e(\underline{x}) - D$. Similarly, the equilibrium rent may have a jump at $\underline{x}$, where $R(\underline{x}^-)$ and $R(\underline{x}^+)$ denote, respectively, the left side and right side limits of $R(x)$ as x approaches $\underline{x}$.

The social cost of a unit increase in $\underline{x}$ is the social contribution of the residents at $\underline{x}$ and this equals the net income minus the consumption of the consumer good, i.e., $C = [y - z(\underline{x})]N(\underline{x}^+) = R(\underline{x}^+)\bar{H}(\underline{x})$, where the second equality is derived from the budget constraint. Thus, the optimal boundary location requires

$$R(\underline{x}^-)\bar{H} + \tau(\underline{x})e(\underline{x}) - D = R(\underline{x}^+)\bar{H}(\underline{x}), \tag{2.10}$$

and land rent has a jump at $\underline{x}$ unless $\tau(\underline{x})e(\underline{x}) = D$.

In Stull's formulation, a unit increase in $\underline{x}$ raises the pollution level at x by $\partial A(x - \underline{x})/\partial \underline{x} = -A'(x - \underline{x})$ and the total social cost of increased pollution is

$$D = \int_{\underline{x}}^{\bar{x}} \frac{\partial U/\partial a}{\partial U/\partial z} N(x)A'(x - \underline{x})\, dx > 0. \tag{2.11}$$

Since, as we have seen, the Pigouvian tax rate is zero in this case, equation (2.10) becomes

$$R(\underline{x}^-) = R(\underline{x}^+) + D/\bar{H}(\underline{x}) > R(\underline{x}^+). \tag{2.12}$$

Thus, land rent jumps at $\underline{x}$ and the residential rent is lower than the industrial rent there. Since the industrial sector outbids the residential sector just outside the boundary, $\underline{x}$, this solution cannot be implemented without some sort of government intervention. Two possible types of interventions have been suggested: one is a land use control which precludes the expansion of the industrial zone, and the other is a differential tax on land depending on land use, with a higher tax rate on industrial use than on residential use.

In Henderson's formulation, a unit increase in x has three effects on the pollution level at x in the residential zone. First, it increases emissions at $\underline{x}$ by $e(\underline{x})$ whose contribution to the pollution level at the CBD boundary is $g(e(\underline{x}), \underline{x}, \underline{x})$. Second, it makes the boundary farther from the existing firms and reduces their contributions to pollution at the boundary by $\partial g(e(x'), x', \underline{x})/\partial \underline{x}$. The sum of these two effects is $[\partial A(E, x, \underline{x})/\partial E][g(e(\underline{x}), \underline{x}, \underline{x}) + \int_0^{\underline{x}} (\partial g(e(x'), x', \underline{x})/\partial \underline{x})\, dx']$. Third, the boundary becomes closer to a resident at x and the pollution level increases by $\partial A(E, x, \underline{x})/\partial \underline{x}$. Thus, the social cost of increased pollution is

$$D = -\left[\int_{\underline{x}}^{\bar{x}} \frac{\partial U/\partial a}{\partial U/\partial z} N(x) \frac{\partial A}{\partial E} dx\right]\left[g(e(\underline{x}), \underline{x}, \underline{x}) + \int_0^{\underline{x}} \frac{\partial g}{\partial \underline{x}} dx'\right] - \int_{\underline{x}}^{\bar{x}} \frac{\partial U/\partial a}{\partial U/\partial z} N(x) \frac{\partial A}{\partial \underline{x}} dx \quad (2.13)$$

Now, it is natural to assume that the contribution of emissions from a firm located at the boundary is equal to the quantity of emissions that it generates, i.e., $g(e(\underline{x}), \underline{x}, \underline{x}) = e(\underline{x})$. Then, $\tau(x) = \tau$ and (2.13) becomes

$$R(\underline{x}^-)\bar{H}(\underline{x}) - \int_0^{\underline{x}} (\partial g/\partial \underline{x})\, dx = R(\underline{x}^+)\bar{H}(\underline{x}) - \int_{\underline{x}}^{\bar{x}} \frac{\partial U/\partial a}{\partial U/\partial z} N(x) \frac{\partial A}{\partial \underline{x}} dx. \quad (2.14)$$

This is the result obtained by Henderson: land rent in general has a jump at $\underline{x}$ but whether it is an upward or downward jump depends on the relative magnitudes of the second terms on the two sides of (2.14). The industrial rent is higher (lower) than the residential rent at the boundary if the social benefit of increased dispersion in the industrial zone due to shifting the boundary farther from the firms is larger (smaller) than the social cost of increased residential pollution caused by moving the boundary closer to residents.

In a special case where the pollution level at x in the residential zone depends only on the total quantity of pollution emissions in the industrial zone and distance from the CBD boundary, $a(x) = A[\int_0^{\underline{x}} e(x')\, dx', x - \underline{x}]$, we have $\partial g/\partial \underline{x} = 0$ and $\partial A/\partial \underline{x} > 0$. Hence, the industrial rent is higher than the residential rent at $\underline{x}$ as in Stull's case: $R(\underline{x}^-) > R(\underline{x}^+)$. This corresponds to the result obtained in Section IV of Helpman and Pines.

Finally, in the symmetric formulation $a(x) = A[\int_0^{\underline{x}} g(e(x'), x - x')\, dx', x]$, the first effect in Henderson's case is present but the second and third effects do not arise, since $\partial g(e, x - x')/\partial \underline{x} = 0$ and $\partial A(E, x)/\partial \underline{x} = 0$. Hence, (2.14) becomes $R(\underline{x}^-) = R(\underline{x}^+)$ and there is no discontinuity in the land rent function. This shows that a jump in land rent profile is caused by a difference in pollution diffusion between the industrial and residential zones. Whether or not such an asymmetry exists is not an economic problem but a technological problem.

In all three cases, the residential rent may increase with distance from the CBD especially in a region close to the CBD boundary. It is easy to see that the rent gradient is

$$\frac{dR(x)}{dx} = -\frac{t}{h(x)} + \frac{\partial U/\partial a}{\partial U/\partial z} a'(x). \tag{2.15}$$

Although the first term on the right side is negative, the second term is positive and as a result, the rent gradient may be positive. As usual, commuting costs tend to make the rent gradient negative, but a location farther from the CBD has less pollution and better environmental quality. If the latter effect is stronger than the former, the rent gradient is positive. In an extreme case where the effect of pollution is very severe, there may be a region where the residential land rent is zero. Such a region is most often a green belt between the industrial and residential zones.

Henderson extended the analysis to the case with more than one city and considered population distribution between cities. The optimal allocation of residents between different cities requires that the social values of marginal residents be equal in all cities. Under the assumption that all individuals receive the same utility level, the social net benefit of a marginal resident is the marginal product of labor minus the value of resources that the resident consumes, i.e., the wages minus the total expenditure, $w-y=s$. Thus, incomes other than wages, s, must be equalized across cities. This solution can be attained if all individuals in all cities own land in all cities equally and obtain an equal share of pollution tax proceeds in all cities. One implication of this result is that a city government should not obtain the tax proceeds. Tax proceeds must be pooled by the central govenment and distributed equally among all individuals.

Helpman and Pines [34] analyzed spatial externalities in a slightly different model. They considered direct quantity regulation in addition to Pigouvian taxes and showed that equilibrium land rent with optimal quantity regulation equals the sum of Pigouvian taxes collected at the location and equilibrium land rent with Pigouvian taxes. They also showed that in a small, open city the optimal solution is attained if the city government chooses Pigouvian taxes (or quantity regulations) so as to maximize the total land rent in the city. This reflects the well-known fact that in a small, open city the benefits of any policy change is perfectly capitalized into a rise in land rent.

Miyao, Shapiro, and Knapp [62] examined the existence, uniqueness, and stability of an equilibrium in a small open city with externalities from producers to residents. They proved the existence of a spatial equilibrium under reasonable assumptions. The uniqueness and stability of the equilibrium, however, may not be obtained, unless the degree of externality is sufficiently small. They showed that if the degree of externality is large, the equilibrium is unstable for certain speeds of adjustment in both the labor and land markets. The instability is caused by the following mechanism. If, due to some perturbations, the industrial zone expands beyond the equilibrium boundary, pollution in the residential zone intensifies because the total quantity of pollution emissions increases. This lowers the residential rent, and if this effect is strong enough, the industrial rent exceeds the residential rent at the new CBD boundary. In such a case a further expansion of the industrial zone occurs and the equilibrium boundary is unstable.

In some cities, air pollution taxes and the quantity regulation of pollution have been implemented. Land use zoning has also been adopted in many cities. These policies are, however, implemented with imperfect information on sources and quantities of pollution emissions. It would be useful to extend the analysis by incorporating incomplete monitoring systems and costs of administering different policy measures. In particular, second-best zoning policies under imperfect pricing of pollution has not been analyzed.

3. EXTERNALITIES AMONG HOUSEHOLDS

Households as well as firms generate externalities which affect other households. First, there may be external economies or diseconomies between different types of people: the rich may fear heavier taxes if poorer households live in the same municipality, whites may have a racial prejudice against blacks, and so on. Especially in the United States, spatial externalities of this type have been extensively analyzed within the context of racial problems. Second, there may be externalities associated with housing upkeep: neighbors of a house receive external benefits from its good maintenance. For example, neighbors can enjoy a beautiful garden, or the neighborhood becomes safer if lighting is provided at night. In this section we consider these two types of externalities between households, although the second type is discussed only briefly.

In models of racial prejudice, it is commonly assumed that whites have an aversion to living near blacks while blacks may or may not prefer to live close to whites. In other words, whites receive external *diseconomies* from blacks living nearby whereas blacks may or may not obtain external *economies* from whites. If white residents publicly display racial prejudice, blacks may also have an aversion to living close to whites and blacks receive external *diseconomies* from whites.

The properties of equilibrium spatial structures resulting from such externalities have been examined in three types of models. The first type, called border models by Yinger [110], *assumes* a completely segregated residential pattern with whites preferring to live away from the white–black border. This type corresponds to Stull's formulation of externalities between producers and households and was adopted by Bailey [6] and Rose-Ackerman [83]. Courant and Yinger [17] criticized this approach on the ground that the segregated pattern must not be assumed but must be derived endogenously. The second type, which were adopted by Yinger [110] and Schnare [90], and called amenity models by Yinger [111], assumes that households are concerned about the racial composition of their own location but not about that of other locations. More specifically, whites living at radius x in a monocentric model are assumed to derive disutility from the proportion of the population at radius x that is black. Whether segregated or integrated residential structure emerges in equilibrium is determined endogenously in such a model. Unfortunately, these models are also restrictive in the sense that households do not care about the race of their neighbors at a slightly different radius. Because spatial externalities are present only at a specific radius, we call models of this type local externality models. The third type, called global externality models, assumes that the total external diseconomies received by a white are the weighted sum of blacks living in the same city where weights are given by a decreasing function of distance between a white and a black. This approach was taken by Yellin [109] and Kanemoto [46, Ch. VI] and corresponds to the symmetric specification in Section 2.

Consider two types of residents, called whites and blacks, in a simplified version of a monocentric city model in Section 2. In order to focus on the spatial distribution of the two types of households, we assume that the CBD is a point, i.e., $\underline{x} = 0$, and the incomes of the two types of households are fixed at y^i, $i = w, b$, where superscipts w and b denote whites and blacks, respectively. We also assume that the city stands ready built so that the lot size, $h(x)$, and the number of households, $N(x)$, at x are exogenously determined, where we assume $h'(x) > 0$ and $N'(x) \geqq 0$, or the lot sizes and the numbers of residents are larger farther from the center.

If the spatial externalities received by a household of type i, $i = w, b$, at x is $a^i(x)$, then the household's utility maximization problem is to maximize the utility function, $U^i(z^i, h(x), a^i(x))$, subject to the budget constraint, $y^i = z^i + R(x)h(x) + t^i(x)$. The bid rent function of households of type i is then $R^i[y^i - t^i(x), h(x), a^i(x), u^i]$. Note that the lot size appears in the bid rent function, since it is exogenously determined.

As noted in the beginning of this section, there are three types of specification of spatial externalities. The first one is the border model which assumes that the strength of externalities depends only on distance from the white–black border, i.e., $a^i(x) = A^i(x - x^*)$, where x^* is the boundary between the white area and the black area. Second, the local externality model assumes that the externalities at radius x depend only on the racial composition at that radius, i.e., $a^i(x) = A^i(N^j(x)/N(x))$, $j \neq i$. Third, the global externality model assumes that the level of externalities received by a household at x is the weighted sum of residents of the other type with weights being a decreasing function of radial distance between households, i.e., $a^i(x) = \int_0^\infty g(|x - x'|)N^j(x')\,dx'$, $j \neq i$, where $g'(\ ) < 0$.

Most of the papers on spatial externalities between households restrict their attention to what might be called passive discrimination, where the well being of discriminators is affected by the locational decisions of others, but discriminators are unable to influence the decisions of others. There is some evidence that this assumption is not satisfied, but, even so, it would be useful to examine what sort of spatial equilibrium emerges only with passive discrimination. See Yinger [111] for a survey of some studies on active discrimination.[2]

The border model assumes a segregated residential pattern, since otherwise the white–black border does not exist and the externality function, $A^i(x - x^*)$, cannot be defined. Given the location of the border, x^*, the slope of the bid rent function is in general

$$\frac{dR^i}{dx} = -\frac{1}{h(x)}\left\{t^{i\prime}(x) - \left[\frac{\partial U^i/\partial h}{\partial U^i/\partial z} - R(x)\right]h'(x) - \frac{\partial U^i/\partial a}{\partial U^i/\partial z}A^{i\prime}(x - x^*)\right\}, \qquad i = w, b. \quad (3.1)$$

The last term in the brace represents the effect of spatial externalities. If blacks live in an inner zone and whites in an outer zone as assumed in Rose-Ackerman, this term is negative for whites and the racial prejudice of whites tends to make their bid rent curve flatter.

We consider only the case where blacks have a steeper bid rent curve than whites in the *absence* of externalities. That is, if the third term is ignored, the bid rent curve of blacks is steeper than that of whites.[3] This is the case considered in most papers and the analysis can be easily extended to other cases. If there are no externalities, the only equilibrium spatial pattern in this case is complete segregation with blacks in an inner zone and whites in an outer zone. In the presence of externalities, however, this is not in general true.

Consider, first, the case where whites are prejudiced against blacks but blacks are neutral. In this case, the equilibrium has the same pattern as the no-externality case. In fact, the racial prejudice makes the pattern more robust, since whites pay a premium for

[2] In a simulation model, King [51] analyzed the effects of restricting the expansion of the black zone by active discrimination. He showed that total land value in the urban areas significantly rises. Landowners, therefore, have an incentive to collude and restrict the area open to blacks.

[3] As shown in Kanemoto [46, p. 184], even if blacks have lower commuting costs, blacks may have a steeper bid rent curve than the whites. The reason is that if whites have a higher marginal rate of substitution between housing and the consumer good than blacks, then whites tend to live in larger houses farther from the center of the city.

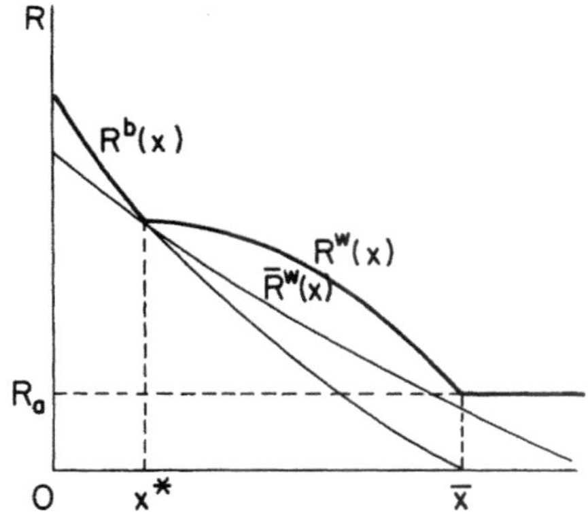

FIGURE 1 The border model with the central location of blacks.

living inside the white area and it becomes more difficult for blacks to enter the white area. This is shown in Figure 1, where $\bar{R}^w(x)$ is the bid rent of whites without externalities and $R^w(x)$ is that with externalities. However, the opposite pattern with whites in an inner zone and blacks in an outer zone may also be an equilibrium if externalities are strong enough. From (3.1), it can be seen that the presence of externalities makes the bid rent curve of whites *steeper* in this case. If this effect is strong enough, the bid rent of whites is higher than that of blacks in the inner zone as in Figure 2. It is not difficult to see that these two patterns are only equilibria.

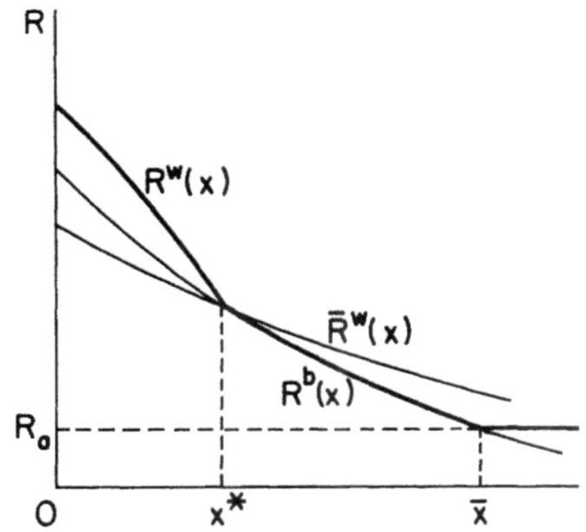

FIGURE 2 The border model with the central location of whites.

As shown by Muth [64, pp. 106–112] and Rose-Ackerman [83], racial prejudice of whites makes whites worse off and blacks better off. Whites who live close to the white–black border suffer simply because they receive external diseconomies. Whites who live far from the border may not receive externalities but they pay higher rent. Blacks become better off because whites now have lower bid rents and rents in the black area become lower. Of course, this result depends on the assumption that discriminition is only passive. If there is active discrimination which prevents the expansion of the black zone, it must be modified.

Courant and Yinger [17] criticized the border model on the ground that segregation is not derived endogenously but simply assumed. They also argued that if there is more than one income class, the model has a serious difficulty. If some of the blacks have much higher incomes than some whites, rich blacks "hop" over poorer whites and the equilibrium solution may involve many black areas. The border model cannot treat a case with more than one black area, since distance from the white–black border cannot be uniquely defined when there is more than one border.

Yinger [110] and Schnare [90] proposed a model which does not have these difficulties. In their local externality model, the level of externalities at a certain radius is a function of the racial composition at that radius only, $a^i(x) = A^i(N^j(x)/N(x)), j \neq i$. Yinger [110] showed that, if blacks have a steeper bid rent curve than whites in the absence of externalities and if only whites are prejudiced, then the only stable equilibrium in the local amenity model is complete segregation with blacks in an inner zone and whites in an outer zone.

Exactly the same result is obtained if blacks as well as whites have negative racial prejudice. Yinger claimed that if blacks prefer racial mixing, neither complete segregation nor complete integration is an equilibrium. Kern [50] pointed out that Yinger's analysis in this case is not correct, since, in a segregated equilibrium, the bid rent curve for both whites and blacks would have discontinuities at the boundary. Moreover, Kern also noted that there is no guarantee that the equilibrium rent profile is continuous as assumed by Yinger. In particular, he showed that:

1) Whenever preference for white neighbors is stronger among

whites than among blacks, integrated equilibrium is unstable, but there is a stable segregated equilibrium.

2) In the opposite case, no segregated equilibrium is possible, but there is a stable integrated equilibrium.

The local externality model assumes that a white household receives externalities only from blacks who live at the same radius. Blacks at any other radii cause no externalities no matter how close they are to the white household. This assumption is quite unrealistic and a more general model, called the global externality model, has been proposed. The global externality model was first developed by Yellin [109]. Although it preceded Yinger [110] and Schnare [90], it did not attract the attention of urban economists primarily because the paper was written using techniques borrowed from the field of physics rather than economics. Another reason is that Yellin analyzed only the optimum allocation.

Kanemoto [46, Ch. VI] examined a market equilibrium in the global externality model. For simplicity, let us first assume that the number of houses per unit distance is constant: $N(x) = N =$ constant. It was shown in Kanemoto [46, Ch. VI] that if whites have racial prejudice and blacks are neutral, then the only equilibrium is complete segregation with the central location of blacks. This result indicates that the existence of externalities does not alter the equilibrium spatial configuration. No active discrimination is, therefore, necessary to confine blacks in the central part of the city. Moreover, racial prejudice makes the segregated pattern more stable, since the bid rent curve of whites becomes flatter.

Even if blacks as well as whites have racial prejudice, the same spatial pattern is an equilibrium. If blacks prefer racial mixing, there is a possibility that this pattern is not an equilibrium. As in the local externality model, the segregated pattern can be an equilibrium if the preference is not too strong.

If the number of houses per unit distance changes with distance from the center, the above result must be modified. This is because the externality function in the global externality model employs only radial distance and circumferential distance does not matter. If, for example, there are more households per unit distance at larger radii, the externality level will be higher at the outer boundary of the black zone than at the inner boundary, which causes an additional tendency to lower the bid rent of whites at the outer boundary.

Finally, it should be noted that the externality level in the global externality model varies continuously over space. In particular, it is continuous at a boundary of a black zone. This may not be realistic. If the externality level is higher at the black side of the boundary than at the white side, the externality level jumps at the boundary. In such a case, the bid rent curve of whites has a jump and the equilibrium rent may be higher at the white side of the border than at the black side.

Rich [78] found that in the Newark metropolitan area of northern New Jersey, blacks pay higher rents than whites at black–white borders and he explained this result noting that blacks are discouraged from locating in white areas by active racial discrimination such as a local vigilante organization and expressions of racial prejudice. This can be interpreted as the case where blacks obtain external diseconomies from whites because of racial prejudice of whites. The above argument can then be applied to the bid rent curve of blacks instead of that of whites, and if there is a jump in externality level at the border, blacks pay higher rents there than whites.

In a model with external diseconomies from one type of household to the other, there is a possibility of dynamic instability: a small increase in the number of blacks in the neighborhood, for example, may drive away all the whites, causing a sudden change in the racial composition.[4] This type of phenomena was analyzed by Schelling [87, 88, 89], Oates, Howrey and Baumol [67], Baumol [7], and Bradford and Kelejian [12], where Schelling called it "neighborhood tipping" and others "a cumulative decay process". The weakness of these earlier works is that individual choice of space and location and the adjustment of land rent are not explicitly considered. Miyao [59], Schnare and MacRae [91], and Kanemoto [47] extended them to incorporate these two elements. Miyao [60] and Anas [1] considered the same problem in the framework of a

[4] Note that this analysis parallels that of Miyao *et al.* [62] which was discussed in Section 2. Our current analysis will be slightly different because we examine the stability of equilibrium in a model with externalities from one household to another rather than producers to households.

probabilistic model of locational choice, and Kanemoto [46] in a monocentric continuous location model.

A cumulative decay process, or a tipping process, involves the following mechanism. An increase in poor households (or blacks) in central cities drives out wealthier residents (or whites) who receive external diseconomies from the poor. The induced emigration of wealthier households to the suburbs causes further deterioration of central cities, and the city deteriorates cumulatively.

As pointed out by Schnare and MacRae [91] and Kanemoto [46, 47], the weakness of this argument is that the adjustment of equilibrium land rent is not explicitly considered. For example, if the land rent falls sufficiently, wealthier people may remain even in the deteriorated central city. For a cumulative process to occur, therefore, there must be something that prevents the land rent from falling.

One possibility is the case where land rent reaches zero. In this case deterioration leads to housing vacancies in the central core. Alternatively, poorer households might support the rent either through an increase in per capita housing demand or through immigration of poorer households from other areas. Most papers consider the latter case, assuming that the city is open.

Now, let us examine the possibility of a cumulative process in the global externality model. Discussions below follow Kanemoto [46, Ch. VI] closely. We assume that the city is open so that migration into and out of the city is free and costless. In this case, the utility levels of whites and blacks then equal those in the rest of the world. The city may not be small, however, and the utility levels may depend on the population of the city. An increase in the population of the city implies a decrease in the population of the outside world, which causes a rise in the utility levels in the outside world because of diminishing returns. We therefore assume that $u^i = V^i(P^i)$ with $V^{i\prime}(P^i) \geqq 0$, $i = w, b$, where u_i and P^i are, respectively, the utility level of a household of type i and the population of type i in the city.

The income of a city resident may also depend on the population of the city and we assume $y^i = y^i(P^i)$ with $y^{i\prime}(P^i) \leqq 0$, $i = w, b$, where y^i is the income of a household of type i. If the city is small compared with the rest of the world, then the utility levels and the income levels are fixed for the city, since they are determined by the conditions in the outside world.

Let x^* denote the white–black boundary. Then the stable equilibrium satisfies

$$P^b(x^*) = \int_0^{x^*} N(x)\,dx \tag{3.2a}$$

$$P^w(x^*) = \int_{x^*}^{\bar{x}(x^*)} N(x)\,dx, \tag{3.2b}$$

where we will see later that the edge of the city, $\bar{x}$, is a function of x^*.

The bid rent functions of blacks and whites can now be expressed as functions of x^*:

$$R^b(x;x^*) = R^b[y^b(P^b(x^*)) - t^b(x), h(x), V^b(P^b(x^*))], \tag{3.3a}$$

$$R^w(x;x^*) = R^w[y^w(P^w(x^*)) - t^w(x), h(x), A^w(x;x^*), V^w(P^w(x^*))], \tag{3.3b}$$

where it is assumed that blacks do not receive externalities and $A^w(x;x^*)$ is the level of externalities received by a white household at x which is defined by

$$A^w(x;x^*) = \int_0^{x^*} g(|x-x'|)N(x')\,dx'. \tag{3.4}$$

At the edge of the city the bid rent of whites must equal the rural rent, $R^w(\bar{x};x^*) = R_a$, which yields $\bar{x} = \bar{x}(x^*)$ and hence $P^w(x^*)$.

If the populations of blacks and whites in the city are fixed, the stability condition for the segregated residential pattern with central location of blacks is that the bid rent curve of blacks is steeper than that of whites at the back–white border,

$$R_x^b(x^*;x^*) \leqq R_x^w(x^*;x^*), \tag{3.5}$$

where $R_x^i(x;x^*) \equiv \partial R^i(x;x^*)/\partial x$. Earlier in this section, we showed that this condition holds. If migration into and out of the city is allowed, however, this condition is not sufficient for stability.

Next, let us introduce the concept of the *boundary* bid rent curve

---

[5] The concept of the boundary bid rent curve was used by Fujita [27] to prove the existence and uniqueness of competitive equilibrium in a monocentric city model. See also a survey article by Fujita in this series.

which is defined as the bid rent at x when the black–white boundary is at x,

$$\hat{R}^i(x) = R^i(x; x), \qquad i = w, b. \tag{3.6}$$

The slope of a boundary bid rent curve is different from that of a bid rent curve, since it includes the effect of a change in the population size associated with a change in the black–white boundary. As shown in Kanemoto [46, Ch. VI], even if the bid rent curve of blacks is steeper than that of whites, the opposite may hold for boundary bid rent curves. The reason is as follows. An increase in the black population associated with an outward movement of the boundary drives up the externality, causing the bid rent of whites to fall. If this effect is very strong, the boundary bid rent curve of whites becomes steeper than that of blacks even though the corresponding bid rent curve is not.

The stability of the black–white border depends crucially on the slopes of the boundary bid rent curves. It is easy to show that, if the boundary bid rent of whites is less steep than that of blacks, then the boundary is stable, and if steeper, then the boundary is unstable. Consider the situation represented by Figure 3b. The boundary is at x^*, and beyond x^* whites outbid blacks. The boundary bid rent of whites is steeper, however, as illustrated in Figure 3a. Notice that, if the boundary x^* is to be an equilibrium, the boundary bid rents must be equal there as well as the bid rents.

Now imagine that the boundary shifts outward to x^* because of some random disturbances. The bid rent of whites falls farther than the bid rent of blacks, as in Figure 3b. Blacks outbid whites at the new boundary and the boundary moves farther outward. The process continues until the boundary reaches x^{**}.

If the boundary had shifted inward, whites would have outbid blacks, causing the boundary to move inward until it reached the center. In this instance x^* is unstable. The same argument applied at x^{**} will show that the boundary is stable at that point.

Although the bid rent curve of whites is flatter than that of blacks, the boundary bid rent curve of whites may be steeper than that of blacks if externalities are strong. In such a case, the black–white boundary is unstable.

Next, consider a historical process in which bid rent shifts up due to some exogenous factors such as technological progress. For

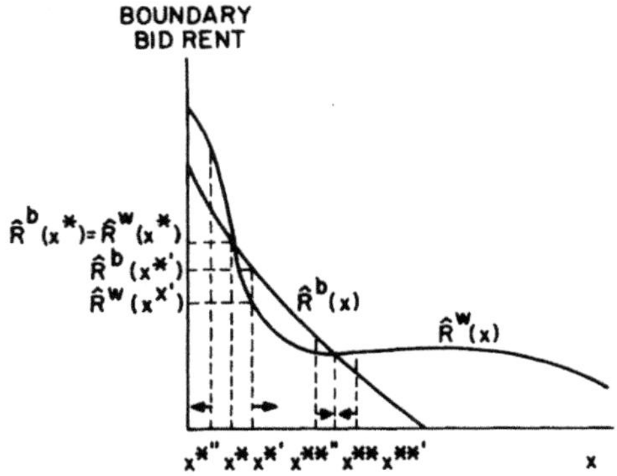

Fig. 3a

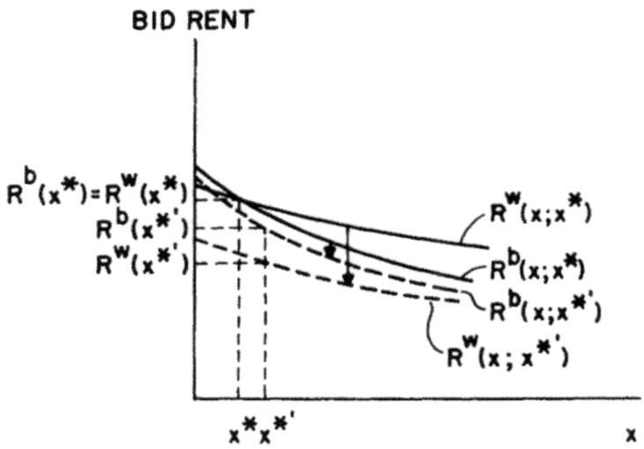

Fig. 3b

FIGURE 3 Stability of boundaries.

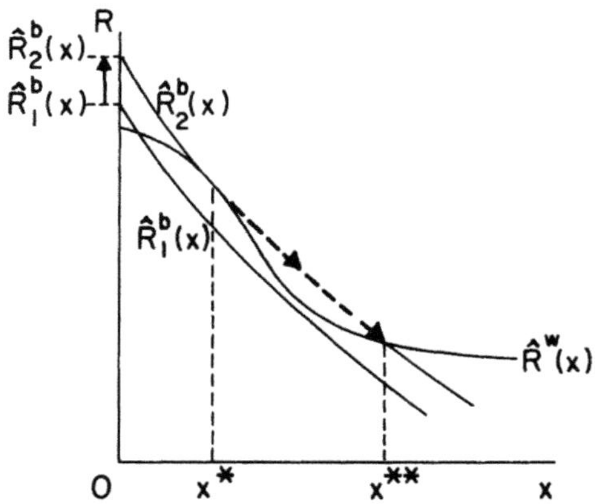

FIGURE 4 A cumulative process.

simplicity, we assume that the bid rent of blacks rises more rapidly than that of whites. An example where the boundary bid rent curve of whites is flatter than that of blacks near the center but becomes steeper at some point is illustrated in Figure 4. In this case, the boundary gradually moves outward until the bid rent of whites becomes tangent to that of blacks, and then jumps to x^{**}.

The cumulative decay process analyzed by Baumol and others can be viewed as a rapid movement of the boundary of the sort described here. If a small increase in the number of blacks lowers the utility level of whites, the whites move out to the suburbs, leading to a further deterioration of central cities. This process occurs only if the rent does not fall sufficiently to compensate whites for the increase in the external diseconomy, or in our model only if the boundary bid rent curve of blacks is flatter than that of whites.

Most of the papers on spatial externalities between households are concerned only with positive issues, but Davis and Whinston [19] and Henderson [36, Ch. 6, Section 2] offer the analysis of the normative side. It is obvious that with spatial externalities a competitive equilibrium is not Pareto optimal. Inefficiency arises in three respects. First, a Pareto optimal allocation requires a Pigouvian tax/subsidy system when externalities exist. Second, the spatial arrangement of households may be suboptimal. A household does not have control over who lives in the neighboring houses and there is no reason to suppose that the equilibrium assignment of households is Pareto optimal. In the special case where external diseconomies are mutual between different types of households, however, there is a tendency for complete segregation as seen earlier in this section and this problem may not arise. Third, as in the case of externalities between producers and households in Section 1, the optimal allocation may require that land rent have a jump at the boundary between different types of households. In such a case, a land use control or a differential tax on land can improve efficiency.

Next, let us turn to housing upkeep externalities. Schall [86] and Stahl [96] analyzed neighborhood externalities arising from maintenance decisions.[6] Good maintenance of a house benefits its

[6] See Henderson [40, Ch. 4] for a more detailed survey of these papers to which our discussion here owes a lot.

neighbors by providing more aesthetic and comfortable neighborhoods. The safety of the neighborhood for both adults and children is also enhanced by repairs of stairways and railings, lighting at night, and salting of sidewalks during the winter time. Since the resident or the owner of a house is not compensated for these externalities, his maintenance expenditure is too low. In order to achieve an efficient allocation, he must be given an extra incentive for better maintenance.

One possible solution is a Pigouvian subsidy. Many of the existing housing subsidy programs, especially a subsidy on home improvement loans, may be justified by this argument.

A second solution is direct regulation of maintenance decisions such as zoning ordinance and building codes. This could be done either by government regulations or by voluntary contracts among residents in the neighborhood.

A third possibility is that housing upkeep externalities can be internalized by concentrating ownership of housing in the neighborhood. This does not happen too often in reality because of a moral hazard problem between renters and owners. If the owner assumes the sole responsibility of maintenance to take advantage of housing upkeep externalities, renters do not have any incentive to keep the maintenance costs low by careful use of the house. Given this situation, the system of owner-occupied housing is usually more efficient than that of concentrated ownership.

Fourth, in stable neighborhoods where neighbors know each other very well, people might recognize the benefit of simultaneously increasing their upkeep. This solution in effect transforms a Nash-type non-cooperative game of competitive equilibrium into some other type such as a cooperative game. Since a cooperative solution is difficult to maintain, various forms of social pressure are applied to prevent nonconforming behavior. This type of solution is probably most common in reality but has not been fully analyzed.

Housing upkeep externalities also affect the timing of redevelopment and reconstruction. When neighborhood housing becomes old, demolition and reconstruction becomes optimal at some point. It does not pay, however, to rebuild only one house when all other houses are decaying. A developer must therefore redevelop the entire neighborhood at the same time, which requires buying up all structures in the neighborhood. This causes the classic holdout problem: people who refuse to sell their houses until the last minute might be able to claim extraordinarily high prices for their houses, since otherwise redevelopment may be impossible. The developer who forsees this problem may refrain from undertaking the development project even when it is socially desirable. This is a justification offered for the use of eminent domain where the government forces the initial owners to sell their houses to the developer (or the government) at "fair" prices. Eminent domain, however, may be politically misused to effectively transfer real income from low income residents of decaying areas to developers and future high income residents. Endorsing the use of eminent domain therefore requires a more careful examination of the severity of the holdout problem and possibilities of misuse.

Finally, if the neighborhood quality and a resident's own maintenance are complements in the utility function of the resident, then multiple equilibria may arise as shown by Schall [86] and Stahl [96]. In the complementarity case, a resident's maintenance expenditure is lower when the neighbors' expenditure is also lower, leading to an equilibrium where everybody maintains a low level of upkeep as well as others with higher levels of upkeep. With multiple equilibria, it is quite possible that the neighborhood is stuck at an equilibrium with very low levels of upkeep even though another equilibrium with higher levels of upkeep is both Pareto superior and locally stable. In such a case, a large scale redevelopment may be able to move the neighborhood to a more efficient equilibrium. This argument may be used to justify government intervention to encourage redevelopment programs. It is, however, very difficult to determine whether or not there actually exists another stable equilibrium with higher levels of upkeep.

4. EXTERNALITIES AMONG PRODUCERS

External economies among producers, often called agglomeration economies, have been considered as one of the major reasons why urban areas exist. Externalities in this context are spatial in the sense that they are associated with proximity between firms, where firms receive external benefits by locating closer to other firms. There have been several papers which explicitly model the spatial aspect of this kind of externality. Pioneering works are Solow and Vickrey [95], Beckmann [9], Cappoza [15], Odland [68, 69], and Borukhov and Hochman [11]. Ogawa and Fujita [70], and Fujita and Ogawa [28] presented more elaborate analyses of equilibrium spatial patterns arising from spatial externalities between firms. An optimal solution of a similar model was analyzed by Imai [42]. Smith and Papageorgiou [93] examined the equilibrium allocation with spatial externalities in a somewhat different model.

The more traditional models of agglomeration economies such as Henderson [35, 36], Kanemoto [46], and Arnott [3] assumed that firms in the same CBD area receive the same amount of external economies regardless of where in the CBD they are located. We first examine this type of models.

Assume, in the model developed in Section 1, that the CBD is a point, $\underline{x}=0$, and that there is no externality from producers to households, $a(x)=0$ for any x. Following Kanemoto [46], we assume that firms obtain external economies from the population size of the city. The production function is $f(N, P_c)$, where N is the number of employees and P_c the population of the city. An increase in population increases the firm's productivity, $f_P \equiv \partial f(N, P_c)/\partial P_c \geqq 0$. This formulation is similar to the models of Marshallian external economies developed by Chipman [16] and further analyzed by Aoki [3] which can result in multi-firm cities when the presence of additional firms is an advantage. If m is the number of firms, the total product of a city is $Y = mf(N, P_c)$ where $m = P_c/N$. We assume increasing average returns to labor when the firm is small, with a gradual shift to decreasing returns as employment increases. This assumption ensures that the optimal firm size is finite.

Consider a flat and fertile plain over which the rural sector is spread out. Cities are sprinkled about on the plain which is so large that the cities do not overlap. Each city consists of a business and production core surrounded by a residential zone. The total population is divided between the urban and rural sectors, where the urban population is further divided among cities.

There are two major choice problems in this model: one determining the allocation of households between the urban and rural sectors and the other choosing the number of cities. First, consider the division of the total population between the urban and rural sectors assuming that the number of cities is fixed. The optimal solution of this problem requires that a Pigouvian subsidy be given to all city residents. A city resident gives external benefits to urban producers through an increase in city population, and should be given a subsidy equal to the value of his marginal contribution to urban production, $s_c = pmf_P$.

If the number of cities is optimally chosen, then the total Pigouvian subsidy in a city equals the total differential rent,

$$s_c P_c = \int_0^{\bar{x}} [R(x) - R_a]\, dx, \tag{4.1}$$

where the differential rent means the difference between the residential rent and the rural rent.

This result suggests that the optimal allocation is a market equilibrium in the following institutional setting. All land is equally and collectively owned by all households in the economy. Residents in a city form a cooperative, or a city government, which rents all the land for the city at the rural rent. Each household, in turn, rents land for housing from the city government, and pays the market-determined rent. Since the urban residential rent is higher than the rural rent, the city government has a surplus revenue. The surplus is returned to city residents as an equal subsidy.

Although the optimal solution is a market equilibrium under this institutional arrangement, the optimal allocation is not a unique market equilibrium as shown by Henderson [35]. A wide range of city sizes greater than the optimum can also be equilibria, and there is no reason to believe that the optimum is likely to be attained.

This point can be illustrated as follows. If we specify the number of cities, a corresponding market equilibrium is obtained and the equilibrium utility level can be written as a function of the population size, $u^*(P_c)$. For simplicity, assume that this function is single-peaked as in Figure 5.

Clearly, city sizes less than P_c^* in Figure 5, where the equilibrium utility level attains its maximum, cannot be stable equilibria. If a household moves to another city, the utility level will rise in the receiving city, and fall in the city which has lost population. Therefore, a household has an incentive to move to another city. The receiving city would continue to grow at least until P_c^* was reached. The losing city would eventually disappear.

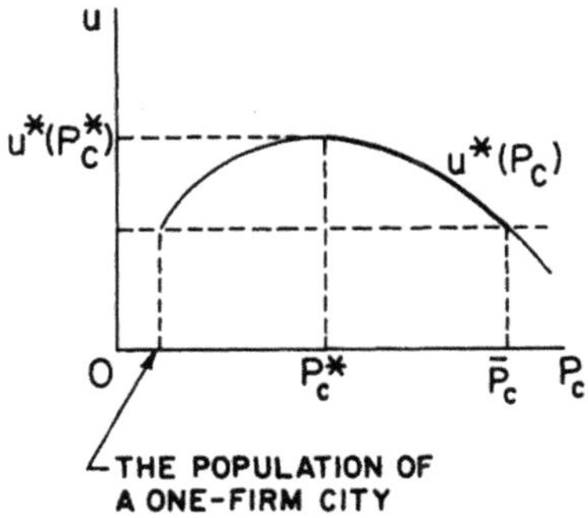

FIGURE 5 Market city sizes.

City sizes greater than P_c^*, however, can be an equilibrium. Households do not have an incentive to move to another city at a city size greater than P_c^* since an increase in the population of the receiving city would lower the utility there. For the same reason they do not have an incentive to move to the rural area, either. The only way, therefore, to reduce the city size is to create a new city. If we do not allow for coalition or entrepreneurship to form a large new city, then all new cities must start from one firm. In this case, a new city will not be formed unless the size of existing cities exceeds P_c^* by so much that the general utility level falls to that of a one-firm city. Therefore, the city sizes between P_c^* and $\bar{P}_c$ tend to remain the same.

Thus, the optimal city size coincides with the minimum of the possible market city sizes, and there is a strong tendency for market city sizes to become too large. This result may justify government intervention to achieve the optimal city size.

Note that this inefficiency result hinges on the fact that a coalition of many firms to form a new city is impossible. If, as assumed by Henderson [36, Ch. 3], there are developers who set up cities and manage land bank companies, this problem will not arise. When all cities are too large, for example, a developer can obtain an extra profit by setting up a city of optimal size and the entrepreneurship of developers restores the optimal city size. In order for the system of city developers to work, however, a developer must be able to buy the city's land at the agricultural price and to lend it to city residents at the residential rent. This may be difficult if the land is initially owned by many small landowners. If a landowner knows that a city is built on the land he owns, he would not sell it at the agricultural price since the land commands a higher price as residential land.

Whether intervention is required or not, the actual situation may be less serious than the model suggests. Historical development has provided us with a hierarchy of cities rather than a single type. Cities produce different sets of commodities, and bigger cities produce more commodities than smaller ones. A new city at a certain level of the hierarchy can be created by adding firms producing new commodities to an existing city at a lower level of the hierarchy. This does not require a very large population shift.

We have assumed that it is the population of a city that generates an external economy. Obviously, this is not the only formulation. For example, we can assume that the total product of a city induces the externality, as in Henderson [35]. In that case, the Pigouvian subsidy should be given to firms as excise subsidy on their product. With this change, the above analysis can be applied and the same conclusions are obtained.

The above analysis can be extended to allow for heterogeneous firms and households if all firms receive external economies from the population size of a city. The major complication is that the assignment of firms and households to particular cities must be determined. This sort of the equilibrium assignment problem has not yet been fully analyzed.[7] Another complication is that cities are no longer identical. The condition for the optimum number of cities must be changed such that the aggregate Pigouvian subsidy equals the aggregate differential rent in a *marginal* city. The equality does not, however, hold in intramarginal cities.[8]

So far the spatial distribution of firms in the CBD is ignored by assuming that the CBD is a point. If the allocation inside the CBD is explicitly modelled, many new issues will arise. For example, there is no guarantee that a city is monocentric. There may be many subcenters, or firms and households are completely mixed so that there is no center. In order to examine these issues, the spatial

---

[7] See Berglas [10] for the analysis of heterogeneous households in a very simple model of local public goods.

[8] See Kanemoto [46, Ch. 2, Section 6] for a more detailed discussion.

nature of externalities between firms must be explicitly modelled. Ogawa and Fujita [70], Fujita and Ogawa [28], and Imai [42] introduced spatial interactions between firms in a linear city version of the spatial equilibrium model.

They all assumed that the productivity of each firm depends on accessibility to all other firms. Specifically, the output of a firm at x is $Q - A(x)$, where Q is assumed to be fixed and $A(x)$ is the cost of spatial interactions with other firms. Ogawa and Fujita [70] and Imai [42] assumed a linear interaction cost function where the total interaction cost for a firm at x is proportional to the sum of distances to all other firms,

$$A(x) = a \int b(y)\, |x - y|\, dy, \tag{4.2}$$

where $b(y)$ is the number of business firms per distance at y and a is a fixed parameter. The formulation of Fujita and Ogawa [28] is equivalent to a nonlinear form,

$$A(x) = a \int b(y)[1 - \exp(-c\, |x - y|)]\, dy, \tag{4.3}$$

where a and c are fixed parameters. In this formulation the interaction cost is a concave function of distance between firms, since, if $f(x) = 1 - \exp(-cx)$, then $f''(x) = -c^2 \exp(-cx) < 0$.

The interaction costs may be interpreted as externalities between firms but another interpretation is also possible. If each firm uses fixed and equal amounts of the products of all other firms as intermediate inputs and if their transportation requires positive costs, then the total transportation cost that a firm must pay can be given by $A(x)$. In this interpretation, the assumption that the firm size is fixed at Q plays an important role. If there is no such indivisibilities and constant (or decreasing) returns to scale prevail, then all activities are spread out evenly over the city. That is, producers of all products have tiny factories at each location, making transportation costs of intermediate inputs zero. Thus, the crucial element in this model is the *combination* of indivisibility in production and interaction costs between firms.

Ogawa and Fujita [70] and Imai [42] have shown that with linear interaction costs the only possible equilibrium land use patterns are: a monocentric configuration where firms are concentrated in the center of the city; a completely mixed configuration where firms and residences are completely mixed; or an incompletely mixed configuration where a mixed zone exists in the center, two residential zones exist in the periphery and business zones exist between the mixed zone and the residential zones. It was also shown that in this case, the equilibrium is unique.

Fujita and Ogawa have also pointed out that the concave cost function case is much more complicated. First, in addition to the three configurations, many other equilibrium configurations such as those with subcenters exist. Second, multiple equilibria are obtained over a wide range of parameter values.

The optimal solution in the linear interaction cost case has been analyzed by Imai [42], where the optimal solution is more concentrated than the equilibrium solution. For example, there are cases where a monocentric configuration is the optimal solution but a completely or incompletely mixed configuration is the market solution. The reason for this result is that the locational decision of a firm has external effects on the interaction costs of other firms. If a firm decides to locate closer to another firm, both firms benefit from a reduction in interaction costs. In making locational decisions, however, a firm does not take into account the benefits to other firms and underconcentration of firms will result. Since interactions between firms are reciprocal, the benefits to other firms equal the savings in interaction costs for the firm and a Pigouvian tax necessary to achieve an efficient allocation exactly equals the actual interaction costs.

Note that externalities of this sort appear only when indivisibility of production is assumed. As explained earlier, in a model of constant (or decreasing) return to scale, all activities are spread out uniformly over the city and there are no interaction costs. Obviously, with no interaction costs, externalities do not arise. In this sense this type of spatial externalities has the same root as that in the locational assignment model of Koopmans and Beckmann [52].

Finally, in the Fujita–Ogawa–Imai model, each firm interacts with all other firms uniformly. This assumption precludes the appearance of spatially separate cities. Although there may be many subcenters, they are all contained in a spatially contiguous city. The reason is obvious: if there is an open space between cities, interaction costs between the two cities can be reduced by moving them closer to each other. In order to carry out the analysis similar to that in the Marshallian externality models of Henderson and Kanemoto, this assumption must be relaxed to include the case where a firm interacts only with some of the firms. One of the most attractive extensions in this direction is to introduce into the Fujita–Ogawa–Imai model the endogenous contact pattern of a firm analyzed in Tauchen and Witte [103, 104].

5. EXTERNALITIES ASSOCIATED WITH URBAN TRANSPORTATION

Urban transportation, especially automobile transportation, is one of the most important sources of external diseconomies in cities. Most of the externalities associated with urban transportation fall in two categories: (1) traffic congestion which represents externalities among travellers, and (2) externalities, such as air pollution and traffic noises, which urban transportation imposes on city residents. This section reviews works on the spatial aspects of both types of externalities.

There are several types of traffic congestion such as flow congestion, queuing congestion, and parking congestion. Flow congestion represents a decrease in the speed caused by an increase in traffic flow. Queuing congestion occurs at an intersection, an entrance to a bridge, or a tollgate when traffic volume is too large. In cities, there may be queues to a parking lot. Among these different types of congestion, flow congestion has been most extensively analyzed and we focus on works on flow congestion in this section. Flow congestion is usually represented by a per capita transportation cost function which depends on the traffic flow and the capacity of the road. Given the capacity, an increase in the traffic flow beyond a certain level slows the speed of traffic and increases both the time and pecuniary cost of transportation.

Traffic congestion has usually been analyzed in non-spatial frameworks. Extending the usual analysis to a spatial model brings up a new problem of determining land use for transportation. The first natural task in a spatial model of traffic congestion is then to characterize the optimal land use pattern. Strotz [99], Solow and

Vickrey [95], Mills and de Ferranti [58], Dixit [21], and many others examined the optimal allocations in models with varying degrees of generality. Some of the more major results of these studies are:

(i) the optimal solution requires congestion tolls to internalize congestion externalities,

(ii) land use between transportation and residence should be determined according to the usual benefit-cost criterion so that a marginal reduction in transportation costs from widening the road equals the cost of doing so, where the latter includes the market land rent, and

(iii) the total receipt of congestion tolls exactly covers the total cost of providing road services (including maintenance costs, construction costs, and land rent) if the transportation cost structure exhibits constant returns to scale, and the total congestion toll is more than (or less than) the total cost of roads if decreasing (or increasing) returns to scale prevail.[9] In the usual formulation, constant returns to scale are obtained when an equally proportional increase in both the traffic flow and the road capacity keeps the per capita transportation costs unchanged.

These results are natural extensions of those obtained in nonspatial models. With transportation congestion, an additional traveller imposes external costs on other travellers by slowing them down. The optimal solution requires congestion tolls to internalize this externality as in result (i). If congestion tolls are set optimally, all the characteristics of the first-best economy with no price distortions are obtained. Thus, results (ii) and (iii) follow.

Although congestion tolls yield an efficient resource allocation, they are difficult to implement because of high administrative costs. It is, therefore, important to consider a second-best problem under the constraint that optimal congestion tolls are not available. In a second-best economy with unpriced (or sub-optimally priced) congestion, the usual benefit-cost criterion obtained in the first-best economy leads to a misallocation of land because market prices no

[9] This result was first obtained by Strotz [99].

longer equal shadow prices. Much of the literature in this area is devoted to the examination of whether or not the naive benefit-cost criterion leads to overinvestment in roads.

The first approach adopted to answer this question is to compare the first-best land use with the market land use under a naive benefit-cost criterion. Legey, Ripper and Varaiya [53], Robson [81], and Kanemoto [45; 46, Ch. IV] showed that the market city has wider roads and is more dispersed than the optimum city.

Although this comparison is much easier to make than a comparison between the second-best city and the market city, its practical usefulness is limited because the first-best city cannot be implemented anyway. A more relevant question is whether or not the market city overinvests in roads compared with the second-best city. Because of the complexity of the second-best solution, however, a direct comparison between the two is difficult. Solow and Vickrey [95], Solow [94], and Kanemoto [43; 44; 45; 46, Ch. V] therefore examined whether or not the naive benefit-cost criterion suggests more investment in roads at the second-best optimum. More specifically, they compared, at the second-best allocation, the savings in transportation costs from widening the road with the cost of doing so.

Arnott and MacKinnon [5] and Arnott [4] extended this approach to an arbitrary land use pattern between transportation and residence. Within this context, the shadow rent on land in residential use does not necessarily equal that in transportation use. For this reason, they explored the relationships between the market rent and the shadow rent for each alternative use.

Finally, direct comparisons between the second-best city and the market city were also carried out by Wan [105] and Pines and Sadka [73], where Wan obtained numerical comparisons in a continuous monocentric city model and Pines and Sadka achieved analytical comparisons in a simple discrete model with only two rings.

When traffic congestion is not optimally priced, the allocation of land between residential and rural uses may also be distorted. Since the market land rent does not necessarily equal the shadow rent, there is no guarantee that the market residential rent at the city boundary reflects the social value of residential land there. An appropriate zoning regulation which controls the boundary of the residential zone will therefore improve the welfare of city residents.

To illustrate these issues, we shall now undertake a spatial analysis of traffic congestion, using a simple two-ring model similar to that of Pines and Sadka [73]. The residential zone is divided into two rings called the center and the suburb, where residents in the suburb must pass through the center to commute to the central business district (CBD). The numbers of residents in the center and the suburb are denoted respectively by N_1 and N_2. Residents in the center incur no commuting costs, but those in the suburb do when they pass through the center. Commuting costs per person per unit period are $g(N_2, T_1)$, where N_2 is the number of residents in the suburb as defined above and T_1 is the amount of land devoted to roads in the center. We assume $\partial g(N_2, T_1)/\partial N_2 \equiv g_N > 0$ and $\partial g(N_2, T_1)/\partial T_1 \equiv g_T < 0$. The first assumption implies that there is congestion, i.e., externality between travellers. The second assumption means that an increase in the amount of land devoted to transportation reduces the commuting costs. Here we ignore construction and maintenance costs of roads and assume that the only input required to produce road services is land.

The total amount of land available in the center is $\bar{L}_1$ which is divided between the residential area, H_1, and roads, T_1, where $H_1 + T_1 = \bar{L}_1$. We assume that no roads are necessary in the suburb so that the suburban area consists only of the residential area, H_2. The amount of residential area in the suburb is an endogenous variable whose opportunity cost is the rural rent, R_a.

All households have the same utility function, $U(z, h)$, and the same income, y. If the commuting cost is t, then a household maximizes the utility function subject to the budget constraint, $y - t = z + Rh$, where R, z, and h denote, respectively, land rent and the amounts of the composite consumer good and residential land. In the same way as in preceding sections, we can define the bid rent function,

$$R(y - t, u) \equiv \max_{\{z,h\}} \{R : y - t = z + Rh,\ U(z, h) = u\},$$

and compensated demand functions of the consumer good and land, $z(R, u)$ and $h(R, u)$. The commuting cost is zero, $t = 0$, for residents in the center and it is $t = g(N_2, T_1) + c$ for those in the suburb, where c represents a toll (or a gasoline tax) which is of course zero if there is no congestion toll. Since all households have the same utility function and the same income, they receive the same utility level in equilibrium.

Consider a closed city with public ownership of land. The population of the city, $N_1 + N_2 = \bar{N}$, is fixed and the differential land rent, which is defined as residential land rent minus the rural rent, is collected by the city government and the rent revenue is equally distributed among all residents in the city. Under the public ownership of land, it is easy to see that the resource constraint for the whole city is

$$w(N_1 + N_2) = z[R(y, u), u]N_1 + z[R(y - t, u), u]N_2 + N_2 g(N_2, T_1) + (\bar{L}_1 + H_2)R_a, \tag{5.1}$$

where w is the per capita production in the city.

The welfare maximization problem of our city is one of maximizing the common utility level, u, under the resource constraint (5.1), land constraints,

$$H_1 = N_1 h(R(y, u), u), \tag{5.2}$$

$$H_2 = N_2 h(R(y - t, u), u), \tag{5.3}$$

$$H_1 + T_1 = \bar{L}_1, \tag{5.4}$$

a population constraint,

$$N_1 + N_2 = \bar{N}, \tag{5.5}$$

and a transportation pricing constraint,

$$g(N_2, T_1) + c = t. \tag{5.6}$$

If zoning of the residential area is impossible, we have an additional constraint that land rent in the suburb equals the rural rent,

$$R(y - t, u) = R_a. \tag{5.7}$$

If the marginal utility of income is strictly positive, the utility maximization problem is equivalent to the resource-surplus maximization problem with the utility level fixed at an optimal level. The latter problem is slightly simpler than the former and yields shadow prices that are easier to interpret. Since the utility level plays no significant role in the surplus maximization problem, we henceforth suppress the variable, u. Assuming an arbitrary land use between transportation and residence, we obtain shadow prices of land in the two uses. Constraint (5.4) can then be ignored and our problem becomes one of maximizing the resource surplus,

$$w(N_1+N_2)-z(R(y))N_1-z(R(y-t))N_2-N_2g(N_2, T_1)-(\bar{L}_1+H_2)R_a,$$

subject to constraints (5.2), (5.3), (5.5), (5.6) in a city with land use zoning. In a city without land use zoning, constraint (5.7) must be added.

First, consider a city with land use zoning which can control the boundary of the residential zone. Depending on the availability of congestion tolls, we have first-best and second-best optima, where the congestion toll, c, is optimally determined in the first-best solution, but it is fixed at zero in the second-best solution with unpriced congestion. Since in reality a gasoline tax serves at least as an imperfect conjestion toll, we also consider a second-best problem with a positive but sub-optimally fixed toll, $c>0$.

In all these optimization problems, first order conditions for endogenous variables, N_1, N_2, t, y, and H_2, must hold. After straightforward manipulations,[10] they become

$$w+\gamma=z_1+\mu_1h_1, \tag{5.8}$$

$$w+\gamma=z_2+\mu_2h_2+g+(N_2-\eta)g_N, \tag{5.9}$$

$$\mu_2=R_2\left(1-\frac{\eta}{N_2e_2}\right), \tag{5.10}$$

$$\mu_H=R_1\left(1-\frac{\eta}{N_1e_1}\right), \tag{5.11}$$

$$\mu_2=R_a, \tag{5.12}$$

where μ_H, μ_2, γ, and η are Lagrange multipliers associated with constraints, (5.2), (5.3), (5.5), and (5.6), respectively, and

$$e_i\equiv-\frac{R_i}{h_i}\frac{dh(R_i)}{dR_i}\geqq 0,$$

[10] Conditions (5.8), (5.9), (5.12) immediately follow from first-order conditions for N_1, N_2, and H_2. Condition (5.10) is obtained from the first-order condition for t and the equality, $z_R+Rh_R=0$, which the compensated demand functions must satisfy. Condition (5.11) is obtained by combining the first-order condition for y with (5.10).

is the compensated price elasticity of demand for residential land in the center ($i=1$) or in the suburb ($i=2$). In order to avoid a degenerate case, we assume that the price elasticity is strictly positive, i.e., $e_i > 0$, $i=1, 2$. This assumption excludes the Leontief type utility function.[11]

Lagrange multipliers, μ_H and μ_2, can be interpreted as the shadow rents of residential land in the center and the suburb, respectively. Conditions (5.10) and (5.11) show that the shadow rents do not equal the market residential rents if the transportation pricing constraint (5.6) is binding, i.e., $\eta \neq 0$. Note that the constraint is binding when the transportation pricing is not optimal. Since the amount of residential land in the suburb can be chosen freely, the shadow rent of residential land in the suburb must equal its opportunity cost, i.e., the rural rent, as in (5.12).

The shadow rent on land in transportation use, which will henceforth be called the shadow rent of the road, is

$$\mu_T = \partial\Lambda/\partial T_1 = -(N_2 - \eta)g_T = B\left(1 - \frac{\eta}{N_2}\right) \tag{5.13}$$

where Λ denotes the Lagrangian for the optimization problem and $B = -N_2 g_T$ is the naive marginal benefit of the road, i.e., a marginal reduction in transportation costs from widening the road. Note that the shadow rent of the road, μ_T, does not equal the naive marginal benefit of the road, B, if the transportation pricing constraint is binding.

Combining (5.8) and (5.9) with the budget constraints, $y = z_1 + R_1 h_1$ and $y = z_2 + R_2 h_2 + c + g$, and noting (5.10) and (5.11) yields

$$c = N_2 g_N - \eta\left[\frac{R_1}{N_2 e_1} + \frac{R_2}{N_2 e_2} + g_N\right]. \tag{5.14}$$

First, consider the first-best solution where the congestion toll, c, is set optimally. The first order condition for c is

$$\eta = 0. \tag{5.15}$$

Thus, from (5.14), the optimal congestion toll is $c = N_2 g_N$ and

[11] Solow and Vickrey [95] and others considered the completely inelastic case. See Kanemoto [46, Ch. V] for a detailed discussion of this case.

equals the marginal externality cost that one commuter imposes on others. Condition (5.15) also implies the standard result in the first-best economy that all the shadow prices equal corresponding market prices: $\mu_H = R_1$, $\mu_T = B$, and $\mu_2 = R_2$. The usual benefit-cost criterion of equating the naive marginal benefit, B, with the market rent, R_1, therefore yields the optimal allocation of land between residential and transportation uses. Since the shadow rent of the residential land in the suburb equals the rural rent from (5.12), the equality of shadow and market rents also implies that there is no need for zoning regulation to achieve the optimal allocation of land between residential and rural uses.

If roads are built optimally, then $R_1 = B$ and hence the total receipt of congestion tolls minus the total market rent of the road is $\pi = cN_2 - R_1T_1 = N_2(N_2g_N + T_1g_T)$, which equals zero when $g(N_2, T_1)$ is homogeneous of degree zero, i.e., the transportation technology exhibits constant returns to scale. This is an extension of the standard result that the profit of a producer with constant-returns-to-scale technology is zero when the marginal cost pricing is adopted. Note also that π is positive in the decreasing-returns case and negative in the increasing-returns case.

Next, consider the second best problem where the congestion toll is zero or fixed at a sub-optimal level. Condition (5.14) then implies that if the toll is lower (higher) than the optimal level, i.e., $c < (>) N_2g_N$, then η is positive (negative). This result is quite natural, since $\eta = \partial\Lambda/\partial c$ is the marginal social benefit of raising the toll. If the actual toll is lower (higher) than the optimal one, then the marginal social benefit of raising the toll must be positive (negative).

We will concentrate on the case where the toll is too low, $c < N_2g_N$. This includes the case of $c = 0$ which has been analyzed most often. It is left to the reader to check that the case with the opposite inequality yields the opposite results. Since $\eta > 0$, conditions (5.11) and (5.13) imply

$$\mu_H > R_1, \tag{5.16}$$

$$\mu_T < B. \tag{5.17}$$

Thus, the naive marginal benefit, B, overestimates the shadow rent of the road, μ_T, and the market residential rent, R_1, underestimates the shadow rent of residential land, μ_H. The naive benefit-cost criterion therefore tends to cause overinvestment in roads.

The result that the naive benefit exceeds the shadow rent is intuitively natural and seems quite general. Since widening the road lowers transportation costs which are already too low, it increases the deadweight loss from incorrect pricing. The shadow rent which includes this effect is smaller than the naive marginal benefit which does not.

The relationship between the market and shadow rents of residential land is more subtle. Since the commuting costs are too low for residents in the suburb, the market rent there is too high relative to that in the center. This however does not explain why the *absolute* level of the market rent in the center is too low as in (5.16) (and that in the suburb is too high). In fact, it can be seen that in a small open city the market rent equals the shadow rent in the center.

Since inequalities, (5.16) and (5.17), hold at any arbitrary road width, it is easy to see that if there is a unique second-best optimum for T_1, then the second-best optimum has less land in transportation use than the market allocation with the naive benefit-cost criterion.

From (5.10) and (5.12), the market rent in the suburb is higher than the rural rent: $R_2 > R_a$. A land use regulation is therefore necessary to prevent the residential area from expanding into the rural area. As noted by Pines and Sadka [73], this result would offer a rationale for a land use control of the residential area adopted in many countries such as Israel, Canada and Japan.

Next, we briefly examine the case where land use zoning is impossible. Without land use zoning, the suburban residential area expands until the market rent there equals the rural rent. This case therefore involves an additional constraint (5.7). Denoting the Lagrange multiplier for this constraint by v, we can obtain the first-order conditions in the same way as before. All conditions except (5.10) remain the same, where (5.10) is replaced by

$$\mu_2 = R_2. \tag{5.10'}$$

Equation (5.14) should accordingly be changed to

$$c = N_2 g_N - \eta\left[\frac{R_1}{N_1 e_1} + g_N\right]. \tag{5.14'}$$

Since $\eta \gtrless 0$ according as $c \lessgtr N_2 g_N$ from (5.14′), all the qualitative results concerning benefit-cost analysis remain the same as before: $\mu_H > R_1$ and $\mu_T < B$ if $c < N_2 g_N$.

So far it has been assumed that only land is used to produce roads, but it is easy to include other inputs such as capital. For example, we can write the transportation cost function as $g(N_2, T_1, K)$, where K denotes the capital input and $g_K \equiv \partial g / \partial K < 0$. Assume that the price of capital is constant at r_K. Then, the shadow price of transportation capital is $\mu_K = \partial \Lambda / \partial K = B_K(1 - \eta / N_2)$, where $B_K = -N_2 g_K$ is the naive marginal benefit of the capital input, i.e., the saving in transportation costs from a marginal increase in capital input. The naive benefit therefore overestimates the true social benefit as in the case of land input. There is no distortion on the cost side, however, and the market price of capital, r_K, equals its shadow price. These results are the same as those obtained by Pines and Sadka [73] who assumed that transportation requires only capital input. Unlike in our model, they assumed that the suburb has a fixed area of land, but this does not change any qualitative results. The only difference is that condition (5.12) no longer holds. Since it plays no role in obtaining our results on comparisons between market and shadow rents, all other results are unchanged.

Most of the work on transportation land use has been carried out in continuous-space models of monocentric cities. In a continuous-space model, the analysis becomes much more complicated because decisions at different locations interact with each other. The qualitative properties of the first-best solution, however, remain the same. At least in the case of zero congestion toll, many of the results in the second-best problem can also be extended. As shown by Arnott [4], the shadow rent of residential land is higher than the market rent near the CBD but the opposite holds near the edge of the city, and the naive benefit of the road exceeds its true social benefit everywhere in the city except at the center where they are equal. The direct comparison between the second-best and market allocation is difficult in a continuous-space model, however, and Wan [105] resorted to numerical examples. His results suggest that the market city tends to devote more land to transportation use than the second-best city.

Kanemoto [43; 44; 46, Ch. V, Section 3] considered a small open city where openness refers to free and costless migration between the city and the rest of the world and smallness refers to the size of the city compared with the rest of the world. In our two-ring model, a small open city is obtained by assuming that both the utility level, u, and the income level, y, are fixed and that the total population of the city is endogenous. The analysis in this case is left to the reader.

Miyao [61] analyzed land use for transportation in a more realistic square city with a grid-type transportation network. An analysis of a still more realistic transportation network, e.g., with a realistic formulation of crossings, would be a fruitful direction of future research.

Wheaton [106] considered a second-best transportation investment problem in a non-spatial model with more than one type of road. He introduced a uniform toll, or a gasoline tax, which does not depend on the congestion level of a particular road. The toll may then be too low in a congested road and too high in an uncongested road. Such a uniform tax has not been analyzed in an explicitly spatial framework.

Since difference between the actual toll and the optimal toll may be interpreted as a commodity tax-subsidy on transportation services, it should also be noted that the second-best transportation investment problem is closely related to the benefit-cost analysis with commodity taxes and/or tariffs examined by Harberger [31], Bruce and Harris [14], Diewert [20], and others.

An interesting departure from the comparison between second-best land use and market land use was undertaken by Wheaton [106] and Wilson [107], where they compared second-best and first-best allocations.

Wheaton showed that a small decline in the toll from the optimal level raises the optimal capacity. Wilson extended this result to show that a large change also raises the optimal capacity under a certain reasonable assumption on the price elasticity of travel demand.

Sullivan [101; 102] performed numerical analyses of an urban general-equilibrium model with traffic congestion that extends the preceding simulation models of Arnott and MacKinnon [5] and Solow [94] to include the spatial allocation inside the CBD.

Most of the spatial models with flow congestion assume that all commuters arrive at the CBD at the same time. Alternatively, commuting congestion can be alleviated by adjusting departure times. Henderson [38] contains the analysis of staggered work hours with endogenous departure times. He showed that congestion externality distorts a commuter's decision on the departure time (or an employer's decision on staggered hours) so that the equilibrium distribution of arrival times is more concentrated than the optimal distribution.

Hatta [33] and Kanemoto [48] analyzed spatial models of mass transit systems. In future, it will become important to introduce modal choice between automobile and mass transit and to analyze the investment criteria for both roads and public transit under unpriced congestion. The cost-benefit analysis of the Victoria line extension to the London Underground System in Foster and Beesly [23] and the analysis of reserved bus lanes by Mohring [63] are pioneering works in this direction. Henderson [35, Ch. 7] also contains the analysis of investment policies in a non-spatial model with modal choice.

Now, we briefly review the second type of externalities associated with urban transportation, such as air pollution and noise. Oron, Pines and Sheshinski [71] and Robson [82] analyzed models where the environmental quality at a certain radius in the city is specified as a function of the traffic volume at that radius. They showed that the market city is larger or more dispersed than the optimum city with a nuisance tax. Robson [82] also examined the effect of pollution produced by residences and obtained the opposite result: the market city without a nuisance tax is too concentrated. Although this comparison is interesting, it might be more useful to identify and analyze relevant policy alternatives in a model with environmental externalities associated with urban transportation.

6. MEASURING THE BENEFITS AND COSTS OF EXTERNALITIES

There have been many attempts at measuring the value of urban externalities. Since by definition no market exists for externalities, no prices can be observed. Hence, the value of externalities can only be measured by indirect methods.

Although several methods have been devised, we review only two methods that have been most extensively used in the field of urban economics.[12] One is based on the hypothesis that the benefits and costs are capitalized into a rise or a fall in land price (or more generally property values), and the other on the hypothesis that they are absorbed by a change in the (real) wage rate.

The capitalization hypothesis, which has been examined by a number of authors, e.g., Polinsky and Shavell [76], Pines and Weiss [74], and Starrett [97], considers the benefits of a public project such as a transportation improvement and a reduction in air pollution and traffic noise. The most important assumption in the hypothesis is that the population of the region affected by the project is endogenous such that migration of households into and out of the region is possible.[13] A public project first benefits residents of the community, but with the possibilty of migration the story does not end here. The project causes immigration of new residents, since the community becomes more attractive. Demand for residential land then rises, which results in a rise in residential land rent. The commercial land rent also rises because firms can now hire workers at a lower wage rate and the marginal product of land rises. This argument suggests that the benefits of a public project are at least partially capitalized into a rise in land rent.

It has been shown that capitalization is perfect in a small open area which satisfies the following assumptions.

1) The area affected by the project is open in the sense that migration into and out of the area is free and costless.

2) The area is small compared with the rest of the economy.

3) There are a sufficient number of identical households.

4) The economy is in long-run equilibrium with free entry of firms.

Assumptions 1, 2, and 3 together imply that the utility levels of the residents cannot change. If the utility level rose, there would be immigration of households and by Assumption 1 immigration would continue until a resident obtains equal utility levels in the area and the rest of the world. But since by Assumptions 2 and 3, any change

[12] See Freeman [26] for other approaches.

[13] It has been emphasized by Stiglitz [98] that the endogeneity of the population size of a community is the most important feature of the theory of *local* public goods.

within the area causes only a negligible change in the utility level in the rest of the world. The public project, therefore, will not affect the utility level of the residents. By Assumption 4, the profits of firms are zero both before and after the project and hence constant. Since neither the residents nor the firms gain from the project, the only place where the benefits can go is to the landowners.[14] Thus, if these four assumptions are satisfied, a change in land rent can be used to measure benefits and costs of externalities.

The capitalization hypothesis is normally applied to a change over time, where the difference between the after-the-project and before-the-project land rent levels reflects the benefits of a project. In practice, however, the assumptions required for perfect capitalization are not often satisfied and a change in land rent does not provide a good approximation of the benefits. Most empirical works, therefore, use cross-sectional (or locational) variation in land rent instead of an over-time change. The capitalization hypothesis can obviously be applied to differences in land rent between regions with different levels of environmental quality if the utility levels and profit levels in the two regions are equalized. If migration between the regions is free and costless, therefore, cross-sectional variation in land rent can be used to measure the benefits of externalities.

Ridker and Henning [79] regressed property values on measures of air pollution and other locational characteristics such as accessibility to highways and school quality, and used the regression coefficients to measure the benefits of pollution abatement. This paper generated a controversy over the interpretation of econometric studies of the relationship between air pollution and property values. The debate was summarized by Polinsky and Shavell [75] and the issue was clarified by Polinsky and Shavell [75, 76] and Freeman [24].

These works are closely related to the hedonic, or characteristics, approach to modelling the market for differentiated products, which

---

[14] If land is collectively owned by all individuals in the entire economy including both the region considered and the rest of the world, then the benefits are spread over all individuals and the utility level of each individual rises by an infinitesimal amount. The sum of benefits over all individuals is, however, finite and equals the increase in the total land rent in the small region. Alternatively, if land within the region is owned by absentee landlords, then the landlords realize the benefits.

was developed by Griliches [30], Rosen [84], and others. The hedonic approach assumes that a differentiated product can be represented by a vector of attributes. The equilibrium price of a commodity is then a function of the attribute vector and the regression carried out by Ridker and Henning [79] can be interpreted as that of the hedonic price function. Theoretical and empirical issues involved in the use of the hedonic approach in measuring environmental benefits are surveyed in Freeman [25, 26].

Let us consider a simple hedonic model to illustrate major issues in the estimation of external benefits from property value data. This approach first assumes that there are many households each of whom buys one house out of many houses with different characteristics. A house can be completely characterized by an attribute vector z which includes the structural, locational and environmental characteristics of the house. A household can also be characterized by an attribute vector, $y = (y_1, y_2, \ldots, y_m)^T = (y_1, s^T)^T$, where y_1 denotes the income, $s = (y_2, \ldots, y_m)^T$ other characteristics such as the age of the head of the family and the number of children, and superscript T a transpose of a vector.

An individual with an attribute vector y has the utility function $U(x, z, s)$ and the budget constraint, $y_1 = x + p^*(z)$, where x denotes the consumption of the composite consumer good and $p^*(z)$ the market price of a house with an attribute vector z. Observing the equilibrium price function, $p^*(z)$, an individual chooses x and z to maximize utility. It is convenient to reformulate this problem in terms of the bid price function. Define $x^*(z, s, \bar{U})$ by identity $U(x^*(z, s, \bar{U}), z, s) \equiv \bar{U}$. Then, the bid price function is $r(z, y, \bar{U}) \equiv y_1 - x^*(z, s, \bar{U})$. The bid price function represents the maximum price that an individual with characteristics y is willing to pay for a house with attributes z at a certain utility level $\bar{U}$.

Figure 6 depicts the relationship between the bid price functions and the equilibrium price function when only the first attribute is variable and all others are fixed. There are many bid price curves of individual y^1 corresponding to different levels of utility. Of course, a lower bid price curve corresponds to a higher utility level. The optimal choice of the attribute is then attained at z_1^1 where a bid price curve is tangent to the equilibrium price curve from below. If there are many households with different attributes, i.e., with different shapes of utility functions and different income levels, then

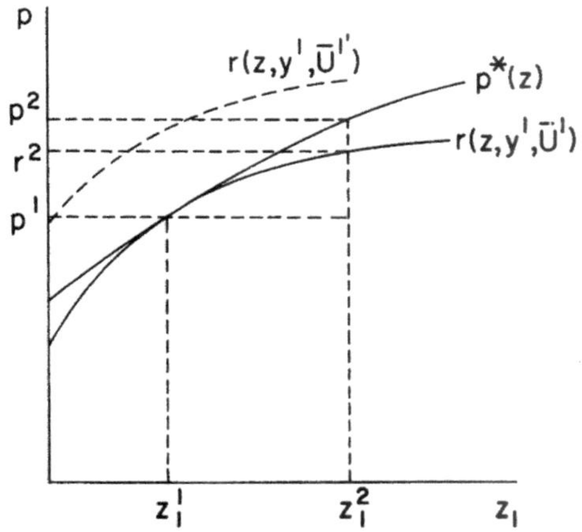

FIGURE 6 The equilibrium price function, the bid price function, and the value of environmental quality.

the equilibrium price function is an upper envelope of their bid price functions.

Now, suppose that attribute z_1 represents the level of environmental quality which is related to air pollution. An improvement of environmental quality from z_1^1 to z_1^2 raises the bid price of household y^1 from $p^1 = r(z^1, y^1, \bar{U}^1)$ to $r^2 = r(z^2, y^1, \bar{U}^1)$. The difference, $r^2 - p^1$, is the maximum amount that this household is willing to pay for the improvement and can be considered as the benefit of the improvement received by the household. Since the benefit, $r^2 - p^1$, is not in general equal to the difference in equilibrium prices, $p^2 - p^1$, the equilibrium price function does not correctly reflect the benefits of environmental quality. Thus, the regression of property values on housing and environmental attributes as in Ridker and Henning [79] does not in general provide a correct estimate of the value of environmental quality. The benefit of an improvement tends to be overestimated, since $p^2 - p^1$ exceeds $r^2 - p^1$ as in Figure 6. It can also be seen from Figure 6 that the cost of a deterioration in environmental quality is underestimated.

As pointed out by Freeman [24], there are two special cases where the equilibrium price function correctly reflects the value of environmental quality. First, since the bid price function and the equilibrium price function are tangent at the optimum point for a household, their slopes are equal there. The equilibrium price function, therefore, yields a correct benefit measure for an infinitesimally small change in environmental quality. Second, if all households have identical utility functions and equal incomes, then they all have the same bid price functions and the equilibrium price function coincides with the bid price function. In this case, too, the equilibrium price function can be used to measure the value of environmental quality. Polinsky and Shavell [76] and Pines and Weiss [74] assumed identical households and considered a marginal change. They naturally obtained the result that cross-sectional differences in land price provide correct measures of the benefits of environmental quality.

If households have different tastes and incomes and if a large change is considered, the equilibrium price function yields a biased estimate of the benefit and the bid price function must be estimated to obtain a correct estimate. The estimation of the bid price function, however, is much more difficult.

Rosen [84] proposed a two-step procedure to estimate structural demand and supply functions for the characteristics of differentiated products. His procedure has been applied to the estimation of the benefit of air quality by Nelson [65] and to the estimation of housing demand functions by many economists such as Witte *et al.* [108] and Linneman [55, 56].

In Rosen's procedure, the equilibrium price function is first estimated by regressing the housing prices on structural, locational and environmental characteristics. If the estimated equilibrium price function is $p = p^*(z)$, the marginal implicit price of a characteristic, $q_i(z)$, $i = 1, \ldots, n$, can be found by differentiating $p^*(z)$ with respect to that characteristic: $q_i(z) = \partial p^*(z)/\partial z_i$. Note that the marginal prices are different for different houses unless the equilibrium price function is linear. In the second step, the inverse demand functions for housing characteristics are estimated by regressing the marginal implicit prices on housing *and* household characteristics. This estimation yields equations of the form,

$$q_i(z) = q_i^D(z, y), \qquad i = 1, \ldots, n,$$

where $q_i^D(z, y)$ is the inverse demand function for attribute i. As noted by Freeman [24, 25], the benefit of a non-marginal change in environmental quality is approximated by the area under the inverse demand curve for the change in question, and aggregate benefits for an urban area are found by summing the benefit measures of all households.

Although Rosen's procedure has been widely used, Brown and Rosen [13] recently described some of the major difficulties in identifying the structureal demand and supply functions. Using an example of a quadratic equilibrium price function and linear inverse demand and supply functions, they showed that Rosen's procedure yields nonsense estimates of demand and supply functions because their estimated coefficients are simple functions of the coefficients of the equilibrium price function and do not provide any more information than that included in the equilibrium price function. Since their criticism relies on special functional forms, its general validity is not quite clear.

Kanemoto and Nakamura [49] clarified the source of the problem and showed that there is a fundamental difficulty in the estimation of structural demand and supply functions in an hedonic model. An hedonic model contains many differentiated products with different characteristics and an equilibrium allocation in the model requires that all of the markets for these products be in equilibrium simultaneously. Then, even though there are many prices in a cross-section data set, we essentially have only one sample of a set of prices that equilibrate all the markets. It is, of course, impossible to estimate structural equations with only one sample.

In order to illustrate this problem, consider the estimation of a bid price function in the completely deterministic case where there are no observation errors, no unobserved attributes, and no specification errors. Suppose that household y obtains the utility level $U^*(y)$ in equilibrium. Then, the bid price function of the household is $r(z, y, U^*(y))$. Since a house is bought by the highest bidder in equilibrium, the equilibrium price of house z must satisfy $p^*(z) = \max_{\{y\}} r(z, y, U^*(y)) = r(z, y^*(z), U^*(y^*(z)))$, where $y^*(z)$ denotes the characteristics of the individual who has the highest bid for z. Thus, the equilibrium price function is an upper envelope of bid price functions of different households.

Since the observed price is the highest bid price among all potential buyers, all the observations lie on the equilibrium locus, $p^*(z)$, in Figure 6. The information contained in the observations is the characteristics of the individual who bought a house with certain characteristics and the price at which it was bought. If, for example, individual y^1 bought house z^1 at price $p^*(z^1)$ as in Figure 6, then we can infer that the bid price curve of the individual is tangent from below to the equilibrium price locus and the slope of the bid price curve at the tangency point z^1 can be found. It is impossible, however, to know the shape of the bid price function at any point other than z^1. Even at z^1, the curvature of the bid price function cannot be known. Thus, the estimation of the bid price function is impossible even in the completely deterministic case.

Since this situation is quite different from the estimation of structural equations in a model of a homogeneous good, the usual identification conditions obtained for the market of a homogeneous good cannot be applied to an hedonic model. In particular, even if the supply of houses is fixed, this does not mean that the bid price function can be identified. Thus, the claim of Harrison and Rubinfeld [32] that a fully identified inverse demand curve can be estimated by regressing equilibrium marginal prices on housing and household attributes if the supply of air quality is perfectly inelastic is not valid for an hedonic model.

As pointed out by Brown and Rosen [13], there are two ways of circumventing this difficulty. One is to use observations from separate markets, e.g., those from spatially distinct markets or a time series of cross-section data. The approach was also suggested by Freeman [24], although in his later paper [25] he seems to imply that Rosen's procedure works even in a single integrated market. If samples are drawn from many segmented markets, there are many equilibrium price functions and the bid price function can be estimated if we are willing to assume that preferences of households do not vary across markets. This case has not been fully analyzed, however, and we still do not know whether or not Rosen's two-step procedure is an appropriate estimation method in this case.

The other way is to impose a priori restrictions on the functional form of the bid price function $r(z, y, \bar{U})$. If the restrictions are strong enough, all parameters of the bid price function may be estimated from the observations only along the equilibrium locus. Quigley [77] took this approach by assuming that the utility function is of the generalized CES form.

In Quigley's model all consumers have the generalized CES utility function,

$$U(x, z) = \sum_{i=1}^{n} \alpha_i z_i^{\beta_i} + x^{\varepsilon},$$

and the utility function is maximized under the budget constraint, $y = x + p^*(z)$, where α_i, β_i are ε are parameters to be estimated. The first order conditions for the utility maximization problem are

$$\log \frac{\partial p^*(z)}{\partial z_i} = \log \frac{\alpha_i \beta_i}{\varepsilon} + (\beta_i - 1) \log z_i - (\varepsilon - 1) \log x,$$
$$i = 1, \ldots, n. \quad (6.1)$$

Quigley proposed the following two-step estimation procedure. First, estimate the equilibrium price function by an appropriate nonlinear estimation technique. Second, compute the partial derivatives of the estimated equilibrium price function for each sample and estimate the first order condition (6.1) using the computed derivatives as dependent variables. The second step estimation yields the estimates of parameters in the utility function, α_i, β_i, and ε.

Even if we accept the restriction of the utility function to the generalized CES form, there are at least two difficulties in Quigley's procedure. First, the functional form of the equilibrium price function must be estimated accurately, since its partial derivatives are used in the second-step estimation. In estimating the first order conditions (6.1), how the partials change as z and x change is crucial and it is not enough to know the approximate *levels* of the partials. The estimated price function must at least provide a good second-order approximation of the true function. If the functional form is misspecified, therefore, the second-step estimation may be seriously biased. Usually, however, the data do not allow us to obtain an accurate estimate of the functional form. For example, in Quigley's estimation the estimated equilibrium price function explains less than 50% of the variations in monthly rents for the sampled dwelling units. In such a case, the confidence intervals are usually too large to yield accurate estimates of the parameters in a sufficiently flexible functional form.

Second, in order to obtain unbiased estimates of parameters, independent variables must not be correlated with the error term. There is, however, a reason to believe that they are correlated in Quigley's estimation method. In econometric studies of housing demand, the major sources of errors are unobserved attributes of houses and individuals because of data limitations. Since the independent variables in the second-step estimation are choice variables for a household, they are affected by (and hence correlated with) unobserved attributes of houses and individuals. The second-step estimation is then likely to be biased.

Kanemoto and Nakamura [49] developed another estimation method which explicitly takes into account unobserved attributes of housing. This method, however, yields biased estimates if there are unobserved attributes of households.

Ellickson [22] developed a multinomial logit model of household bids for dwelling units, treating the bid prices of households as random variables. Lerman and Kern [54] extended this model by making use of observable information on the price paid by the winning bidder. The extended specification makes it possible to estimate the bid price function. This approach is attractive because the bid price function can be estimated directly without estimating the equilibrium price function. At this stage, however, it is not clear whether or not it provides a fully identified bid price function.

Next, consider an alternative method for measuring urban externalities which uses variations in wage rate instead of property values.[15] This approach has been applied mostly to differences in amenities between cities, whereas the one based on property values has been more often applied to different locations in a certain city. According to Rosen [85, p. 75], an intuitive justification of this approach is:

> Those cities exhibiting negatively valued attributes such as high crime rates and extensive pollution must also offer higher wages and lower prices of housing services to induce workers to locate there. Conversely, cities embodying the more preferred attributes will offer lower wage rates and the higher site values as in-migration increases the labor supply in those locations relative to the demand for it and also increases the demand for living space. The differences in wages and living costs between cities with different attributes are in fact the prices that signal the proper assignments by choking off demand for preferred locations and impelling people to live in less desirable places because it is cheaper to do so.

In order to make the argument more precise, let us consider households which are faced with a problem of relocating to a different city. All households have identical ability and an identical utility function, $U(x, h, z)$, where x is the consumption good, h is the amount of space occupied, and z is amenities specific to a city.

[15] Nordhaus and Tobin [66] pioneered this approach.

Let $r(z)$ and $w(z)$ denote land rent and wage rate at a city with amenities z. The budget constraint for a household is then $w(z) = x + r(z)h$, where the consumption good is taken as numeraire and non-wage income is ignored. The indirect utility function is then

$$V(r, w, z) = \max_{\{x, h\}} \{U(x, h, z) \colon w = z + rh\}.$$

Since all households are identical, they must receive the same utility level in equilibrium. Hence, $V(r(z), w(z), z) = u = \text{const}$. Consider two cities whose amenity levels are different only by an infinitesimal amount. The difference between them can be represented by

$$0 = \frac{du}{dz} = V_r \frac{dr}{dz} + V_w \frac{dw}{dz} + V_z,$$

where subscripts, r, w, and z, represent partial derivatives of the indirect utility function. By Roy's Identity and the envelope theorem, the above equality can be rewritten as

$$\frac{U_z}{U_x} = -h\frac{dr}{dz} + \frac{dw}{dz}. \tag{6.2}$$

The left side is the marginal rate of substitution between amenities and the consumption good which can be interpreted as the marginal benefit of amenities. Equation (6.2) shows that the marginal benefit of amenities does not equal a difference in residential land rent or a difference in wage rate, but equals a combination of these two. Note that the capitalization hypothesis discussed earlier in this section still holds if rental price of land in production use is included, since a difference in wage rate induces a difference in land rent *in production use*.

Rosen [85] developed a theoretical foundation for his approach using an unconventional definition of real wage, i.e., the wage rate divided by land rent, w/r, but his empirical study uses the conventional one, i.e., the wage rate divided by a cost-of-living index.[16] It turns out that the conventional definition provides a

---

[16] See Henderson [39] for another attempt at justifying the wage-based approach.

more straightforward theoretical foundation. The cost-of-living index is the cost of a fixed representative bundle of goods that a household purcheses. Thus, in our context it is $c(r) \equiv x + hr$ with *fixed x* and *h*. A difference in *real* wage rate is then

$$\frac{d}{dz}(w(z)/c(z))) = \frac{w}{c^2}\left[\frac{c}{w}\frac{dw}{dz} - \frac{h\,dr}{dz}\right]$$

$$= -h\frac{dr}{dz} + \frac{dw}{dz} = \frac{U_z}{U_x} \quad \text{if} \quad w = c. \qquad (6.3)$$

Thus, if the cost-of-living is defined so that it equals the wage rate initially, a difference in real wage rate equals the value of amenities.

Note that this argument applies only to an infinitesimally small difference in amenities. For a finite difference, we encounter the usual index number problem in choosing the correct cost-of-living index and a difference in real wage rate in general yields only an approximation to the true benefit of amenities. Furthermore, if households are not identical, we have another difficulty similar to that discussed earlier in the property value approach.

If a proper cost-of-living index can be found for different locations, the above approach is very convenient, since a single-equation regression yields at least an approximate measure of the value of amenities. In many cases, however, it is difficult to find good data on the costs of living in different locations. Also, approximation may not be good for a finite difference in amenities. Some authors, such as Getz and Huang [29] and Cropper [18], took the approach of building a model of cities by specifying explicit forms of utility and production functions and estimating their parameters by a simultaneous regression of structural equations in the model. A shortcoming of this simultaneous estimation approach is that because of the complexity of the model, it only permits very simple functional forms such as the Cobb–Douglas form. The possibility of extending their methods to more flexible functional forms must be explored. It is also left for future research to compare the performances of different approaches.

References

[1] Anas, A., "A Model of Residential Change and Neighborhood Tipping," *Journal of Urban Economics,* **7** (1980), 358–370.

[2] Aoki, M., "Marshallian External Economies and Optimal Tax Subsidy Structure," *Econometrica,* **39** (1971), 35–54.
[3] Arnott, R., "Optimal City Size in a Spatial Economy," *Journal of Urban Economics,* **6** (1979), 65–89.
[4] Arnott, R., "Unpriced Transport Congestion," *Journal of Economic Theory,* **21** (1979), 294–316.
[5] Arnott, R. J. and J. G. McKinnon, "Market and Shadow Land Rents with Congestion," *American Economic Review,* **68** (1978), 588–600.
[6] Bailey, M. J., "Note on the Economics of Residential Zoning and Urban Renewal," *Land Economics,* **35** (1959), 288–292.
[7] Baumol, W. J., "Macroeconomics of Unbalanced Growth," *American Economic Review,* **62** (1972), 415–426.
[8] Baumol, W. J., "The Dynamics of Urban Problems and Its Policy Implications," in *Essays in Honours of Lord Robbins,* ed. by Peston and Corry. New York: International Arts and Sciences Press, 1972.
[9] Beckmann, M. J., "Spatial Equilibrium in the Dispersed City." in *Mathematical Land Use Theory,* ed. by G. J. Papageorgious. Lexington, MA: Lexington Books, 1976.
[10] Berglas, E., "Distribution of Tastes and Skills and the Provision of Local Public Goods," *Journal of Public Economics,* **6** (1976), 409–423.
[11] Borukhov, E. and O. Hochman, "Optimum and Market Equilibrium in a Model of a City without a Predetermined Center," *Environment and Planning A,* **9** (1977), 849–856.
[12] Bradford, D. F. and H. H. Kelejian, "An Econometric Model of the Flight to the Suburbs," *Journal of Political Economy,* **81** (1973), 566–589.
[13] Brown, J. N. and H. S. Rosen, "On the Estimation of Structural Hedonic Price Models," *Econometrica,* **50** (1982), 765–768.
[14] Bruce, N. and R. Harris, "Cost-Benefit Criteria and the Compensation Principle in Evaluating Small Projects," *Journal of Political Economy,* **90** (1982), 755–776.
[15] Capozza, D. R., "Employment-Population Ratios in Urban Areas: A Model of the Urban Land, Labor and Good Markets," in *Mathematical Land Use Theory,* ed. by G. J. Papageorgious. Lexington, MA: Lexington Books, 1976.
[16] Chipman, J. S., "External Economies of Scale and Competitive Equilibrium," *Quarterly Journal of Economics,* **86** (1970), 347–385.
[17] Courant, P. N. and J. Yinger, "On Models of Racial Prejudice and Urban Residential Structure," *Journal of Urban Economics,* **4** (1977), 272–291.
[18] Cropper, M. L., "The Value of Urban Amenities," *Journal of Regional Science,* **21** (1981), 359–374.
[19] Davis, O. A. and A. B. Winston, "The Economics of Complex Systems: The Case of Municipal Zoning," *Kyklos,* **17** (1964), 419–445.
[20] Diewert, W. E., "Cost-Benefit Analysis and Project Evaluation: A Comparison of Alternative Approaches," *Journal of Public Economics,* 22 (1983), 265–302.
[21] Dixit, A., "The Optimum Factory Town," *The Bell Journal of Economics and Management Science,* **4** (1973), 637–651.
[22] Ellickson, B., "An Alternative Test of the Hedonic Theory of Housing Markets," *Journal of Urban Economics,* **9** (1981), 56–79.
[23] Foster, C. D. and M. E. Beesley, "Estimating the Social Benefit of Constructing an Underground Railway in London," *Journal of the Royal Statistical Society,* series A126 (1963), 46–92.
[24] Freeman, A. M. III., "On Estimating Air Pollution Control Benefits from

Land Value Studies," *Journal of Environmental Economics and Management,* **1** (1974), 74–83.

[25] Freeman, A. M. III, "Hedonic Prices, Property Values and Measuring Environmental Benefits: A Survey of the Issues," *Scandinavian Journal of Economics,* **81** (1979), 154–173.

[26] Freeman, A. M. III, *The Benefits of Environmental Improvements.* Baltimore: Johns Hopkins University Press, 1979.

[27] Fujita, M., "Existence and Uniqueness of Equilibrium and Optimal Land Use: Boundary Rent Curve Approach," Working Paper in Regional Science and Transportation No. 89, University of Pennsylvania, 1984.

[28] Fujita, M. and H. Ogawa, "Multiple Equilibria and Structural Transition of Non-Monocentric Urban Configurations," *Regional Science and Urban Economics,* **12** (1982), 161–196.

[29] Getz, M. and Y. Huang, "Consumer Revealed Preference for Environmental Goods," *Review of Economics and Statistics,* **60** (1978), 449–458.

[30] Griliches, A., *Price Indexes and Quality Change: Studies in New Methods of Measurement.* Cambridge, Mass.: Harvard University Press, 1971.

[31] Harberger, A. C., "Three Basic Postulates for Applied Welfare Economics: Interpretive Essay," *Journal of Economic Literature,* **9** (1971), 785–803.

[32] Harrison, D. Jr. and D. L. Rubinfeld, "Hedonic Housing Prices and the Demand for Clean Air," *Journal of Environmental Economics and Management,* **5** (1978), 81–102.

[33] Hatta, T., "Competition and Nationally Optimum Resource Allocation under the Presence of Urban Traffic Congestion," *Journal of Urban Economics,* **14** (1983), 145–167.

[34] Helpman, E. and D. Pines, "Optimal Zoning and Corrective Taxation in a System of Open Cities," Working Paper No. 90, Foerder Institute of Economics Research, Tel-Aviv Univesity, 1976.

[35] Henderson, J. V., "The Sizes and Types of Cities," *American Economic Review,* **64** (1974), 640–657.

[36] Henderson, J. V., *Economic Theory and the Cities.* New York: Academic Press, 1977.

[37] Henderson, J. V., "Externalities in a Spatial Context: The Case of Air Pollution," *Journal of Public Economics,* **7** (1977), 89–110.

[38] Henderson, J. V., "The Economics of Staggered Work Hours," *Journal of Urban Economics,* **9** (1981), 349–364.

[39] Henderson, J. V., "Evaluating Consumer Amenities and Interregional Welfare Differences," *Journal of Urban Economics,* **11** (1982), 32–59.

[40] Henderson, J. V., *Economic Theory and the Cities,* Second Edition, New York: Academic Press, forthcoming.

[41] Hochman, O. and H. Ofek, "A Theory of the Behavior of Municipal Governments: The Case of Internalizing Pollution Externalities," *Journal of Urban Economics,* **6** (1979), 416–431.

[42] Imai, H., "CBD Hypothesis and Economies of Agglomeration," *Journal of Economic Theory,* **28** (1982), 275–299.

[43] Kanemoto, Y., "Congestion and Cost-Benefit Analysis in Cities," *Journal of Urban Economics,* **2** (1975), 246–264.

[44] Kanemoto, Y., "Optimum, Market and Second-Best Land Use Patterns in a von Thünen City with Congestion," *Regional Science and Urban Economics,* **6** (1976), 23–32.

[45] Kanemoto, Y., "Cost-Benefit Analysis and the Second Best Land Use for Transportation," *Journal of Urban Economics,* **4** (1977), 483–503.

[46] Kanemoto, Y., *Theories of Urban Externalities,* Amsterdam: North-Holland, 1980.
[47] Kanemoto, Y., "Externality, Migration, and Urban Crises," *Journal of Urban Economics,* **8** (1980), 150–164.
[48] Kanemoto, Y., "Pricing and Investment Policies in a System of Competitive Commuter Railways," *Review of Economic Studies,* **51** (1984), 665–681.
[49] Kanemoto, Y. and R. Nakamura, "A New Approach to the Estimation of Structural Equations in Hedonic Models, *Journal of Urban Economics,* **19** (1986), 218–233.
[50] Kern, C. R., "Racial Prejudice and Residential Segregation: The Yinger Model Revisited," *Journal of Urban Economics,* **10** (1981), 164–172.
[51] King, A. T., "General Equilibrium with Externalities: A Computational Method and Urban Applications," *Journal of Urban Economics,* **7** (1980), 84–101.
[52] Koopmans, T. C. and M. J. Beckmann, "Assignment Problems and the Location of Economic Activities," *Econometrica,* **25** (1957), 53–76.
[53] Legey, L., M. Ripper and P. Varaiya, "Effect of Congestion on the Shape of a City," *Journal of Economic Theory,* **6** (1973), 162–179.
[54] Lerman, S. R. and C. R. Kern, "Hedonic Theory, Bid Rents, and Willingness-to-Pay: Some Extensions of Ellickson's Results," *Journal of Urban Economics,* **13** (1983), 358–363.
[55] Linneman, P., "Some Empirical Results on the Nature of the Hedonic Price Function for the Urban Housing Market," *Journal of Urban Economics,* **8** (1980), 47–68.
[56] Linneman, P., "The Demand for Residence Site Characteristics," *Journal of Urban Economics,* **9** (1981), 129–148.
[57] Livesey, D. A., "Optimum City Size: A Minimum Congestion Cost Approach," *Journal of Economic Theory,* **6** (1973), 144–161.
[58] Mills, E. S. and D. M. De Ferranti, "Market Choices and Optimum City Sizes," *American Economic Review,* **61** (1971), 340–345.
[59] Miyao, T., "Dynamic Instability of a Mixed City in the Presence of Neighborhood Externalities," *American Economic Review,* **68** (1978), 454–463.
[60] Miyao, T., "A Probabilistic Model of Location Choice with Neighborhood Effects," *Journal of Economic Theory,* **19** (1978), 357–368.
[61] Miyao, T., "A Note on Land Use in a Square City," *Regional Science and Urban Economics,* **8** (1978), 371–379.
[62] Miyao, R., P. Shapiro and D. Knapp, "On the Existence, Uniqueness and Stability of Spatial Equilibrium in an Open City with Externalities," *Journal of Urban Economics,* **8** (1980), 139–149.
[63] Mohring, H., "The Benefits of Reserved Bus Lanes, Mass Transit Subsidies, and Marginal Cost Pricing in Alleviating Traffic Congestion," in *Current Issues in Urban Economics,* ed. by P. Mieszkowski and M. Straszheim. Baltimore: Johns Hopkins University Press, 1979.
[64] Muth, R. F., *Cities and Housing,* Chicago, University of Chicago Press, 1969.
[65] Nelson, J. P., "Residential Choice, Hedonic Prices, and the Demand for Urban Air Quality," *Journal of Urban Economics,* **5** (1978), 357–369.
[66] Nordhaus, W. and J. Tobin, "Is Growth Obsolete?" in *Economic Growth,* New York: National Bureau of Economic Research, 1972.
[67] Oates, W. E., E. P. Howrey and W. J. Baumol, "The Analysis of Public Policy in Urban Dynamic Models," *Journal of Political Economy,* **79** (1971), 142–153.

[68] Odland, J., "The Spatial Arrangement of Urban Activities: A Simultaneous Location Model," *Environment and Planning A,* **8** (1976), 779–791.
[69] Odland, J., "The Conditions for Multi-Center Cities," *Economic Geography,* **54** (1978), 234–244.
[70] Ogawa, H. and M. Fujita, "Equilibrium Land Use Patterns in a Non-monocentric City," *Journal of Regional Science,* **20** (1980), 455–475.
[71] Oron, Y., D. Pines and E. Sheshinski, "Optimum vs. Equilibrium Land Use Patterns and Congestion Toll," *The Bell Journal of Economics and Management Science,* **4** (1973), 619–636.
[72] Oron, Y., D. Pines and E. Sheshinski, "The Effect of Nuisances Associated with Urban Traffic on Suburbanization and Land Values," *Journal of Urban Economics,* **1** (1974), 382–394.
[73] Pines, D. and E. Sadka, "Optimum, Second-Best, and Market Allocations of Resources within an Urban Area," *Journal of Urban Economics,* **9** (1981), 173–189.
[74] Pines, D. and Y. Weiss, "Land Improvement Projects and Land Values," *Journal of Urban Economics,* **3** (1976), 1–13.
[75] Polinsky, A. M. and S. Shavell, "The Air Pollution and Property Value Debate," *Review of Economics and Statistics,* **57** (1975), 100–104.
[76] Polinsky, A. M. and S. Shavell, "Amenities and Property Values in a Model of an Urban Area," *Journal of Public Economics,* **5** (1976), 119–129.
[77] Quigley, J. M., "Nonlinear Budget Constraints and Consumer Demand: An Application to Public Programs for Residential Housing," *Journal of Urban Economics,* **12** (1982), 177–201.
[78] Rich, J. M., "Municipal Boundaries in a Discriminatory Housing Market: An Example of Racial Leapfrogging," *Urban Studies,* **21** (1984), 31–40.
[79] Ridker, R. G. and J. A. Henning, "The Determinants of Residential Property Values with Special Reference to Air Pollution," *Review of Economics and Statistics,* **49** (1967), 246–256.
[80] Riley, J., "Optimal Residential Density and Road Transportation," *Journal of Urban Economics,* **1** (1974), 230–249.
[81] Robson, A., "Cost-Benefit Analysis and the Use of Urban Land for Transportation," *Journal of Urban Economics,* **3** (1976), 180–191.
[82] Robson, A., "Two Models of Urban Air Pollution," *Journal of Urban Economics,* **3** (1976), 264–284.
[83] Rose-Ackerman, S., "Racism and Urban Structure," *Journal of Urban Economics,* **2** (1975), 85–103.
[84] Rosen, S., "Hedonic Prices and Implicit Markets, Product Differentiation in Pure Competition," *Journal of Political Economy,* **82** (1974), 34–55.
[85] Rosen, S., "Wage-Based Indexes of Urban Quality of Life," in *Current Issues in Urban Economics,* ed. by P. Mieszkowski and M. Straszheim. Baltimore: Johns Hopkins University Press, 1979.
[86] Schall, L. D., "Urban Renewal Policy and Economic Efficiency," *American Economic Review,* **66** (1976), 612–628.
[87] Schelling, T. C., "Models of Segregation," *American Economic Review,* **56** (1969), 488–493.
[88] Schelling, T. C., "Dynamic Models of Segregation," *Journal of Mathematical Sociology,* **1** (1971), 143–186.
[89] Schelling, T. C., "A Process of Residential Segregation: Neighborhood Tipping," in *Racial Discrimination in Economic Life,* ed., by A. H. Pascal. Lexington, Mass.: Lexington Books, 1972.
[90] Schnare, A. B., "Racial and Ethnic Price Differentials in an Urban Housing Market," *Urban Studies,* **13** (1976), 107–120.

[91] Schnare, A. B. and C. D. MacRae, "The Dynamics of Neighborhood Change," *Urban Studies,* **15** (1978), 327–331.

[92] Sheshinski, E., "Congestion and the Optimum City Size," *American Economic Review,* **63** (1973), 61–66.

[93] Smith, T. R. and G. T. Papageorgiou, "Spatial Externalities and the Stability of Interacting Populations Near the Center of a Large Area," *Journal of Regional Science,* **22** (1982), 1–18.

[94] Solow, R. M., "Congestion Cost and the Use of Land for Streets," *The Bell Journal of Economics and Management Science,* **4** (1973), 602–618.

[95] Solow, R. M. and W. S. Vickrey: "Land Use in a Long Narrow City," *Journal of Economic Theory,* **3** (1971), 430–447.

[96] Stahl, K., "Externalities and Housing Unit Maintenance," Discussion Paper No. 80–22, Institute of Business and Economic Research, University of California, Berkeley, 1980.

[97] Starrett, D. A., "Land Value Capitalization in Local Public Finance," *Journal of Political Economy,* 89 (1981), 306–327.

[98] Stiglitz, J. E., "The Theory of Local Public Goods," in *The Economics of Public Services,* ed. by M. S. Feldstein and R. P. Inman. London: Macmillan, 1977.

[99] Strotz, R. H., "Urban Transportation Parables," in *Public Economy of Urban Communities,* ed. by J. Margolis. Baltimore: Johns Hopkins University Press, 1965.

[100] Stull, W. J., "Land Use and Zoning in an Urban Economy," *American Economic Review,* **64** (1974), 337–347.

[101] Sullivan, A. M., "The General Equilibrium Effects of Congestion Externalities," *Journal of Urban Economics,* **14** (1983), 80–104.

[102] Sullivan, A. M., "Second-Best Policies for Congestion Externalities," *Journal of Urban Economics,* **14** (1983), 105–123.

[103] Tauchen, H. and A. D. White, "An Equilibrium Model of Office Location and Contact Patterns," *Environment and Planning A,* **15** (1983), 1311–1326.

[104] Tauchen, H. and A. D. White, "Social Optimal and Equilibrium Distributions of Office Activity: Models with Exogenous and Endogenous Contacts," *Journal of Urban Economics,* **5** (1984), 66–86.

[105] Wan, F. Y. M., "Accurate Solutions for the Second-Best Land Use Problem," Technical Report No. 79–30, Institute of Applied Mathematics and Statistics, University of British Columbia, 1979.

[106] Wheaton, W. C., "Price Induced Distortion in American Highway Investment," *Bell Journal of Economics* **9** (1978), 622–632.

[107] Wilson, J. D., "Optimal Road Capacity in the Presence of Unpriced Congestion," *Journal of Urban Economics,* **13** (1983), 337–357.

[108] White, A. D., H. J. Sumka and H. Erekson, "An Estimate of a Structural Hedonic Model of the Housing Market: An Application of Rosen's Theory of Implicit Markets," *Econometrica,* **47** (1979), 1151–1173.

[109] Yellin, J., "Urban Population Distribution, Family Income and Social Prejudice," *Journal of Urban Economics,* **1** (1974), 21–47.

[110] Yinger, J., "Racial Prejudice and Racial Residential Segregation in an Urban Model," *Journal of Urban Economics,* **3** (1976), 383–396.

[111] Yinger, J., "Prejudice and Discrimination in the Urban Housing Market," in *Current Issues in Urban Economics,* ed. by P. Mieszkowski and M. Straszheim. Baltimore: Johns Hopkins University Press, 1979.

INDEX

For Product Safety Concerns and Information please contact our EU representative GPSR@taylorandfrancis.com
Taylor & Francis Verlag GmbH, Kaufingerstraße 24, 80331 München, Germany

www.ingramcontent.com/pod-product-compliance
Ingram Content Group UK Ltd.
Pitfield, Milton Keynes, MK11 3LW, UK
UKHW021957180926
475701UK00003B/67

* 9 7 8 0 4 1 5 8 6 6 3 3 0 *